Sweets without Sinning

Gwyneth Dover

with Richard Dover

Photography by Mostafa Hammuri

SIDGWICK & JACKSON
LONDON

I would like to dedicate this book to Richard, Mum, Dad and two very good friends of ours: Josie and Stewart. Richard, as usual, has been extremely supportive and hasn't minded testing the recipes too much! My Mum and Dad have been patient, loving and very helpful – especially in the very traumatic periods. Josie and Stewart have been good enough friends to give honest criticism of the book and have therefore added new dimensions to my writing. I thank them all for giving me the confidence and love I need.

First published in Great Britain in 1990 by
Sidgwick & Jackson Limited

Copyright © 1990 Gwyneth and Richard Dover

Reprinted August 1990 (twice)

Designed by Geoff Hayes
Cartoons drawn by Margaret Goodwin
based on ideas supplied by
Gwyneth and Richard Dover

All photographs styled by the author.

ISBN 0 283 06021 2

Typeset by Macmillan Production Limited
Printed and bound in Great Britain by
Butler & Tanner Ltd, Frome and London

for Sidgwick & Jackson Limited
1 Tavistock Chambers, Bloomsbury Way
London WC1A 2SG

Contents

Acknowledgements   vi

Introduction   **Don't Dessert Your Heart**
Our inspirational story about fighting heart
disease– and winning   1

Chapter One   **The Food Connection**
Why is the food we eat a health hazard?   5

Chapter Two   **Cupboard Love**
The ingredients explained and substitution
charts given   9

Chapter Three   **A Word About The Recipes**   21

Chapter Four   **Playing the Fool**
Delicious fools, mousses and whips   25

Chapter Five   **Feeling Fruity**
Fruits of the season – wild and cultivated –
imaginatively presented to destroy the 'boring
fruit salad' syndrome   41

Chapter Six   **Fromage to Cheesecake**
Amazing healthy, low calorie cheesecakes
which look, and taste, absolutely wonderful   59

Chapter Seven   **Filo Fantasies**
Unusual and impressive desserts using filo
pastry   75

Chapter Eight   **Frozen Assets**
Refreshing ice creams and sorbets to tempt the
taste buds   85

Chapter Nine   **The Proof is in the Pudding**
Familiar favourites that everyone loves   97

Chapter Ten   **Tempting Tarts**
Mouthwatering tarts that melt in the mouth   111

Chapter Eleven   **Saucy Toppers**
Sauces to drizzle over your healthy desserts   121

Index   127

Acknowledgements

The stunning photographs in *Sweets Without Sinning* are due to the talents of the photographer Mostafa Hammuri. You really feel as though you could eat the sweets off the pages, don't you? I thank him sincerely for his perfectionism, patience and good humour.

I would also like to thank Jennifer of Recollections, 76, The High Street, Skipton, North Yorkshire, for providing the exquisite antique china for the photographs. Needless to say I was reluctant to return the pieces as they were so nice.

The many guests who have stayed with us at Harrow Ings earn a big thank you as well – for they are the people, as well as Richard, my Mum and my Dad, who have been guinea pigs for the desserts. Without their co-operation and comments I would not have been able to write the book.

Introduction
Don't Dessert Your Heart

In 1987, when my husband Richard and I became the first winners of the 'Here's to Health Award', we were greeted by a barrage of photo sessions. For hours in the Embankment Gardens in London we leapt off benches, threw our feet in the air, jumped and smiled gamely – all the while holding our luminescent white satin rosettes which claimed to the world that we were the winners of *Here's Health* magazine's competition for the healthiest couple in the UK. On that sunny April day, we certainly felt like it!

As Richard romped through the park, lifting and spinning me like a twenty-year old man, I couldn't help but remember the man of sixteen years ago – a thirty-five year old who was too weak to peel an orange.

For those of you who don't know our story, Richard and I were married on 31 August 1974. Serious heart disease had plagued Richard and his family for many years and Richard had a blood cholesterol level over four times the norm. His heart was enlarged, a valve leaked and he had advanced arteriosclerosis which resulted in crippling angina pains between the shoulder blades. By the age of thirty-five, he had already suffered three major heart attacks. He was lucky to be alive – and, unbeknown to us, the doctors considered him a lost cause.

The drugs that the medical profession prescribed had terrible side effects. We decided to take matters into our own hands – and that's where our fight began. I spent more and more hours in medical libraries searching over any information relevant to health and diet. Labelled 'cranks', I nonetheless persisted – and the result paid off. Armed with my new-found knowledge I altered our lives drastically.

Richard had not always been so ill. In fact, until he was thirty-five, he was a normal, healthy young man (or at least so he thought) who was climbing the corporate ladder rapidly in a career in insurance. I suppose he was what many people would have called a 'whiz kid'. He enjoyed a very full and active life. He played golf regularly, was an avid gardener and enjoyed 'Do It Yourself' around the home.

Each day was packed with activities. Richard could not have imagined, in his wildest nightmares, what was in store for him.

Suddenly, like a bolt out of the blue, Richard was struck down with a major heart attack which was quickly followed by two smaller ones. He was extremely lucky to have survived. People always seem to expect warning signs but in most cases, as in Richard's, there simply aren't any. One minute you're fit and healthy and the next minute you are a heart-attack victim; one of the many statistics. Everyone who knew Richard was shocked. He was only in his mid-thirties and was not, by any stretch of the imagination, overweight.

Our lives were being subtly changed by Richard's heart disease. He now found it increasingly difficult to play the game of pitch and putt, which had been reluctantly swapped for the golf he so loved. The recuperation stops he needed became more frequent and lengthy. Eventually we stopped playing the game altogether. Richard found it embarrassing to have to stop on the course in the middle of playing a hole while other people waited to either tee off or play through. The problem is that if people can't actually see a disability, as with heart disease, they assume that you are all right and just wasting time or larking about.

Even the relatively simple task of shopping became fraught with problems as Richard became more incapacitated. He used to pretend to stop and look in shop windows until the pain subsided a little then walk slowly on, hoping that no passers-by had noticed. Stairs became a nightmare as each single step became a Mount Everest to him. It was a major problem if the lift or escalator in a store or multi-storey car park was out of order and, of course, they very often are.

We were made to stop and think about every single thing that ordinary people took for granted. I don't thing anyone really appreciates good health until it's too late. One day you have it and the next day you don't. It's as simple and as cruel as that.

The deterioration in Richard's health after his heart attacks was fairly gradual at first and at the time we didn't really notice the changes taking place. It was when we stepped back and took stock of the situation that we realized just how restricted he had become. Most of the things we enjoyed doing together like gardening, walking, golfing and just general pottering, we found almost impossible.

In March 1978 Richard had the triple coronary bypass operation he had waited almost a year for. The hospital's 'cold list' hadn't claimed him as the doctors had predicted. And, what's more, he not only survived the operation that had an 80 per cent chance of killing him, but he made a full and rapid recovery. This was a second bite of life's cherry.

A stumbling block that I could see clearly was Richard's very high and dangerous cholesterol level. The prescribed 'cholesterol-controlling' drugs had no beneficial effect whatsoever. We persuaded the doctors to take Richard off these drugs and to monitor him with just dietary changes. This was before the days when the medical profession agreed that cholesterol was a major factor in heart disease and could be diet related.

Our 'normal' diet contained too much fat, sugar, salt and not enough fibre. This is where my research came into play. Anything containing saturated fat was banned from the house; and that meant making all the food myself so that I had control over what we ate. Sugar and salt were minimized and our fibre intake dramatically increased by eating more cereals, wholegrains and pulses, etc.

Within a few weeks Richard's cholesterol level was down for the first time to normal and it remained there. He was carefully monitored for a year and then discharged. And this transformation was entirely without drugs, just diet. The doctors and specialists were amazed at the results.

Even the cholesterol deposits, those creamy-coloured lumps under the skin that accumulate around the eyes, had disappeared completely. The deposits which had formed large lumps on the tendons in his hands and ankles had also vanished. It was not only possible to avoid high cholesterol levels but also the make the condition regress. This meant that Richard's arteries would remain clear of the cholesterol deposits that caused the initial problem – that narrowed the artery walls and restricted the blood supply.

Today people just don't believe that Richard had heart disease. Someone once said of Richard that he was the greatest comeback since Lazurus – and it's true. Not many men of Richard's age, let alone with his health problems, would even dream of buying a massive, derelict old barn to convert themselves. Richard not only dreamt it – he did it. Of course he had a jolly good apprentice – me!

We bought the property in October 1982 and started to convert in early 1983. We learnt by trial and error as neither of us has a building background. In the summer of 1983 we decided to knock all the holes through the two-feet-thick stone walls for the windows on the ground floor. We thought that we would be able to weatherproof them with frames and glazing before the arrival of winter. We didn't. Piles of snow filled the barn and gales blew throughout the entire winter. I have never felt as cold in my entire life.

We had to do everything from scratch. All of the window and door openings had to be created; walls, ceilings and floors all had to be built; and then there was the plastering. To be capable of working from early in the morning to very late at night (often after midnight) on such heavy projects, you must be fit and healthy. We must be gluttons for punishment because early this year we decided to convert our shepherd's cottage from a 'shell' into three more *en suite* bedrooms. To see Richard clambering up scaffolding, building the roof trusses and laying the heavy stone roof slates is wonderful. He never ceases to amaze people – me included!

We opened up 'Harrow Ings' to guests in 1987 and it keeps us both very busy. Life is never dull or boring at our house – every single minute is spoken for. We serve traditional and healthy breakfasts and hardly ever bully people into trying the healthy alternatives – except on those couple of occasions when I have discovered a guest with a heart problem! We are gaining quite a reputation for our breakfasts and now have over forty different meals which we serve at various times. And I'm not going to tell you what they are – you'll have to come and try them for yourself!

Richard is still as fit as a lop. To those not familiar with this Yorkshire term, it means flea. In fact, on the very strenuous publicity tour for my first book *A Diet For Life* he wore everyone out. One signing session had gone a little awry because of a publicity mix-up in the newspapers and nobody knew I was there. Richard decided to do something about it. He promptly made a sandwich board of two showcard displays promoting my book. Popping it over his shoulders, he, to the disbelief of the shop assistants, proceeded to walk around the shopping centre in the luminous green and white boards. The unfortunate thing was that the cardboard was extremely thick and didn't bend under pressure – which led to Richard becoming firmly stuck in a telephone box. Luckily the centre was busy and passers-by helped to free him. I was worried that he would get arrested. But how's that for determination and im-provisation?

Richard had pestered me for years to write a book on practical, healthy eating but I was too involved in my career as a financial economics lecturer even to contemplate it. Then we won the award and it changed our lives. We were swamped with letters, telephone calls and callers at our home all wanting information. People in the media were telling me to write a book and there was an obvious need for one. I left my full-time job to concentrate on writing. The result was *A Diet For Life*. The success of that book and the response I had from the public led me to write this one. We are a nation of sweet lovers and people were constantly asking for healthy dessert recipes. So here you have it – a book chock full of delicious, healthy, and low calorie desserts.

Chapter One
The Food Connection

Remember the saying that was very popular a few years ago: 'a moment on the lips, forever on the hips'? Well, that philosophy is probably far more accurate of sweets than of anything else. Fortunately that is no longer the case. No more do you have to feel guilty when you indulge yourself in a rich and creamy dessert – now you can eat 'sweets without sinning'.

I know from my own experience that when I have ordered a sweet in a restaurant, the moment I started to eat it I felt at least two sizes larger! It's incredible, isn't it? When we arrived home I would say to Richard that I felt fat, would pester him by asking repeatedly "Do I look any bigger?" I would then stare into a full-length mirror, assessing the possible damage to the shape before me.

Sweets have become, to the figure conscious and those concerned with their health, either a boring fruit salad with a spoonful of yoghurt – if you're lucky – or a more elaborate dessert which is banished to become an occasional 'treat'. It's such a shame because I very firmly believe that food should be enjoyed and that this is true of sweets more that anything else. The problem is that our traditional sweets are loaded with sugar, saturated fat, cholesterol and those dreaded calories – all the things of which we, as a nation, are supposed to be reducing our consumption. As such, sweets are not only a hazard to our health but they also substantially increase our padding – and most of us have enough of that already. So the reputation that sweets have of being the most unhealthy part of any meal is probably well deserved. But that no longer means altogether abandoning sweets in favour of an apple. After all, why throw the baby out with the bathwater?

The thing to remember about our Western diet is that we consume far too much fat – especially the 'bad' saturated type, far too much sugar, far too much salt and nowhere near enough fibre. Research carried out all over the world shows us that by instituting changes to our diet we would drastically reduce the incidence of killers like heart disease and many forms of cancer. In this country people seem to expect to suffer from blood pressure, arthritis and strokes. It's just a natural part of growing older. But in other societies, where diets are much healthier, such diseases are unheard of. We should not think of these diseases as inevitable but as avoidable.

The best known of the recent studies on diet and disease carried out in this country are the NACNE (National Advisory Committee On Nutritional Education) Report, published in 1983, and the COMA (Committee On The Medical Aspects Of Food Policy) Report, published in 1984. Both of these reports caused quite a stir because they actually state that our eating habits are causing serious health problems which can be avoided. A strong recommendation to reduce our fat, sugar and salt intake was made, along with the suggestion that we increase the amount of fibre we consume. Our eating habits need to be changed – and that is official. A very crucial point brought out by the reports is that everyone is at risk with the British diet – not just those people with a family history of heart disease. Whether you are a child, an old age pensioner, male or female – you are at risk. It's certainly food for thought, isn't it?

I know that it's very easy to convince yourself that somehow you are immune to contracting cancer or suffering a heart attack. But believe me you are not. No one is. At the moment you may feel fit and healthy and illness may be the last thing on your mind. But, more often that not, these diseases do not give warning signs. You only have to walk around a heart or cancer ward in a hospital to realize the truth of this statement.

The remark that I most frequently hear from people is that they "have an uncle who smoked over sixty cigarettes a day, ate a full English breakfast without fail each morning, drank and didn't exercise. He died when he was ninety-eight years old."

Does this sound familiar to you? Well, there are exceptions to every rule and this gentleman is clearly one of them. What you have to remember is that statistical research from Britain and other countries shows the true picture. In 1988, one Briton died every three minutes from heart disease. Heart disease alone prematurely kills three in ten of all men and two in ten of all women. And that's just heart disease. In this country 180,000 deaths are caused each and every year by that one killer disease. It is this overall trend which must be examined and not the odd exceptions – because that's all they are, exceptions.

While other countries like the USA, Australia, Finland and Belgium have done something about the 'epidemic', we in Britain have done very little. The result is that while the incidence of heart disease and cancer has fallen dramatically in these other countries, ours is still rising. Britain now has one of the highest heart disease and stroke rates in the entire world.

People often say to me that it seems like something is good for you one minute and the next it's bad – so why bother at all? It is true that the information on healthy eating is not static – but then neither is research or there would be no point to it. The problem lies in the fact that we are given snippets of information now and then instead of being given the full story. This form of education can not only be very confusing but also quite misleading. The basic message, however, remains the same. As we learn increasingly more about the topic of healthy eating, each little change to our diet can only do good. For example, a few years ago we were told fibre was good for you; now we know that there are different types of fibre which all perform different and important functions. Research has progressed to the stage that more and more details are becoming available all the time.

We had one guest staying at Harrow Ings last year who was recovering from a heart attack and was probably going home to bypass surgery. This chap wanted a full traditional English breakfast and I was, to say the least, reluctant to indulge him. I tried to talk him into trying a healthy alternative breakfast but he just wouldn't hear of it. His argument was that he may go out tomorrow and get run over by a bus or killed in a car crash. I must admit that this kind of attitude finds no sympathy with me at all. It's certainly true that any one of us could go out tomorrow and be killed. Obviously, you will still minimize the risk of this happening by looking both ways before you cross the road – and not dashing out just as a big double-decker approached. Nor will you drive the wrong way down the fast lane of the motorway. Sensible precautions can be applied in the same way to eating habits. You can minimize the risk of contracting major diseases by eating a healthier balance of foods. And that, for me, is what it's all about. No one can tell you that by changing your diet you will be 100 per cent protected from major disease, but it will substantially reduce the risk factor. And, besides, you're worth it, aren't you?

It's all very well for me, or anyone else for that matter, to suggest that you change your diet to one that is low in fat, sugar and salt and high in fibre. But, at the end of the day, it's you who has to make the changes and naturally the adjustment is very often easier said than done. All too often it is simply assumed that you know how to make the changes. Unless we are given the facts, in a clear way, and are shown how to implement the necessary changes, in both a practical and enjoyable way, how can we expect to make any changes at all? That is precisely what my books aim to do.

An important note. A healthy diet is crucial in achieving and maintaining good health. However, it is also important to make the rest of your life as healthy as you can. If you smoke, stop. If you lack exercise then begin to exercise gently each day. Try to reduce the stress in your life and learn how to cope with it more effectively. All these factors play an important role in good health.

Chapter Two
Cupboard Love

This book is packed full of delicious desserts that are not only remarkably low in calories but are good for you as well. Many will see this as a contradiction in terms – but I assure you it doesn't have to be, sweets can play a positive role in the modern diet, contributing important vitamins, minerals and fibre while being low in fat and sugar. By now you probably have an image in your mind of a boring wedge of melon with a glacé cherry perched precariously on top – or an earthenware dish full of granola. How unappetizing they both sound! These are the stereotypes of healthy, low calorie sweets that *Sweets Without Sinning* completely destroys.

Using the same successful formula as in my first book *A Diet For Life*, I transform the most unhealthy, calorie-filled recipes into healthier, slimline versions of the same delicious thing. The process is simple and foolproof because all you have to do is swap the unhealthy ingredients for healthier ones. The ingredients we want to avoid are those that are high in fat (especially saturated) and sugar, and low in fibre. This process automatically reduces substantially the calorie content – without making the dessert tasteless. Therefore you can enjoy ice creams and cheesecakes in the knowledge that they are actually doing your body some good – and not piling on the inches. And, what's more, you will find the adapted recipes actually taste far nicer than the original sugar-laden treats.

You don't have to disjoint your eating habits and throw everything into reverse. If you attempted to make all the changes at once you would probably give up after a week or two. The idea is to make short and long-term changes that you can be happy with for the rest of your life. It has, therefore, to be both practical and enjoyable. And that doesn't mean a life of abstinence and dull, boring food. In this book you will find deliciously rich cheesecakes which are low in calories, creamy ice creams that melt in the mouth and low-fat pastry treats. Once you become familiar with swapping the ingredients around it will seem like second nature to you. Remember, however, that shopping may take a little longer at first because you will be searching for ingredients that are unfamiliar to you. As with any change to your lifestyle the adoption of well-balanced eating habits takes a little more time initially but after that, healthy cooking takes no longer than traditional.

Many proponents of healthy eating put forward very extreme diets – their interpretation of an 'ideal' diet. And that's all very well for some people, some of the time. The problem with this is that anything taken on in an extreme form tends to be only temporary, just a 'fad'. Eating is fun; it's a social activity and not just a function we perform to survive. Food is a pleasure to be enjoyed – especially sweets.

The important thing is a movement towards a healthier way of eating. There is nothing wrong in a good old compromise. If you can't live with pastry made with 100 per cent wholemeal flour then try 50 per cent wholemeal and 50 per cent white flour. That, in my book (no pun intended) is far better than rejecting entirely the whole healthy eating idea because you can't live with it. It has to be practical for you. After all, some change is far better than no change at all.

You will find that some of the ingredients I use may be unfamiliar to you but don't let that put you off. Most of them are readily available from the larger supermarkets or from your local healthshop. One of the exciting aspects about trying different foods is the fun you have tracking down the ingredients and stocking up your cupboard with new things.

You will find the ingredients upon which so many of our traditional desserts are based are absent or minimized in my recipes. Ingredients such as cream, full fat soft cheese, sugar, butter, egg yolks and chocolate have been replaced by healthier alternatives. The following will give you some idea of those ingredients that should be avoided, made minimal or swapped for a healthier substitute. You should also get into the habit of regularly reading the labels on the foods you intend to buy. You would be very surprised at the amount of added sugar and fat in many items. It is becoming easier to avoid these invisible 'baddies' as low sugar and low fat foods are increasingly making appearances on our supermarket shelves. A word of caution: don't be fooled by the manufacturers' claims when they state things like 'lower in sugar' or 'lower in fat' – lower than what! These statements are very misleading and really don't mean very much at all. You have to read the labels and, if in doubt, contact the manufacturer.

Ingredients to avoid	Why?	The Healthier Alternatives
Dairy cream – all types	High saturated fat, cholesterol, and calories. (Double cream is 48 per cent fat.)	Tofu, low fat yoghurt and *fromage frais*.
Non-dairy cream substitutes	High in saturated fat, cholesterol and calories.	Tofu, low fat yoghurt and *fromage frais*.
Commercial dairy and non-dairy ice cream	High in saturated fat, cholesterol and calories.	Home-made ice cream using healthy ingredients.
Egg yolks	High in saturated fat, cholesterol and calories.	Extra egg whites.
Full cream milk	High in saturated fat and cholesterol.	Skimmed milk or soya milk.

Ingredients to Avoid	Why?	The Healthier Alternatives
Semi-skimmed milk	High in saturated fat, cholesterol and calories. Better than full cream milk but higher in saturated fat, cholesterol and calories than skimmed.	Skimmed milk or soya milk.
Evaporated or condensed milk	High in saturated fat, cholesterol, sugar and calories. (Many condensed milks are over 55% sugar.)	Tofu, *fromage frais* and low fat yoghurt.
Full fat yoghurt	High in saturated fat, cholesterol and calories.	Low fat natural yoghurt.
Fruit-flavoured yoghurt	High in saturated fat, cholesterol, sugar and calories.	Low fat natural yoghurt, liquidized with fresh fruit.
Full fat cream and soft cheese	High in saturated fat, cholesterol and calories.	Low fat soft and cream cheese, quark, low fat cottage cheese and ricotta cheese.
Butter	High in saturated fat, and cholesterol.	Unhydrogenated, polyunsaturated margarine.
Suet	High in saturated fat, and cholesterol.	Unhydrogenated, polyunsaturated margarine.
Lard	High in saturated fat and cholesterol.	Unhydrogenated, polyunsaturated margarine.
Hydrogenated margarine	High in saturated fat and cholesterol.	Unhydrogenated, polyunsaturated margarine.

Ingredients to Avoid	Why?	The Healthier Alternatives
Chocolate	High in saturated fat and cholesterol, sugar and calories.	Carob 'chocolate'.
Cocoa powder	High in saturated fat, cholesterol, sugar and calories.	Carob powder.
Sugar	Empty calories.	Fruit juice, concentrated fruit juice, fresh fruit, dried fruit, sweet cicely, angelica and honey.
Canned fruit in syrup	High in sugar and calories.	Fruit: fresh, dried or canned in its own juices.
Pie fillings	High in sugar and calories.	Fresh and dried fruit.
Sugared cereals	High in sugar and calories.	Sugar-free cereals.
Biscuits	High in saturated fat, cholesterol, sugar and calories.	Home-made biscuits and wholewheat cereal biscuits.
Packaged cake mixes	High in saturated fat, cholesterol, sugar and calories.	Home-made cakes using healthy ingredients.
Commercially baked goods	High in saturated fat, cholesterol, sugar and calories.	Home-made goods using healthy ingredients.
Coconut, Brazil nuts, cashew nuts	High in saturated fat, and triglycerides. (Coconut is about 66% fat.)	Sunflower, pumpkin, sesame seeds, walnuts and almonds.
Refined flours, eg. white	Low in fibre.	Wholemeal flour.

Ingredients to Avoid	Why?	The Healthier Alternatives
Self-raising flour	High sodium content.	Plain flour.
Baking powder	High sodium content.	Low sodium baking powder.
Coconut oil	High saturated fat.	Safflower oil.
Palm oil	High saturated fat.	Sunflower oil.
Vegetable oil	High saturated fat.	Olive oil.
Blended oils	High saturated fat.	Soyabean, walnut oil and sesame seed oil.

Now let's have a closer look at some of those ingredients that you may not have used much before.

Tofu

Tofu is a soft bean curd made from the soya bean and has been served as a staple food in the Far East for over 2,000 years. The West has been slow to recognize both the benefits and versatility of this amazing food. It used to be available only from healthshops but it is now making an appearance on supermarket shelves everywhere – so we may see an increase in its use.

Tofu, although it sounds and looks rather unpromising, does have a lot going for it. It contains none of the 'baddies' associated with our Western diet but many of the 'goodies'. It is described by many as the 'perfect' food, and I agree. It is a rich and efficient source of protein as well as being high in calcium, iron and nutrients. At the same time it's very low in fat with no cholesterol at all. And, what's more, it contains only 70 calories per 100 grams. That makes it an invaluable addition to anyone's diet.

The taste of tofu is very bland, making it ideal for any kind of cooking as it's perfect for sweet as well as savoury dishes. It takes on the flavour you add to it. You can buy tofu in various forms such as firm, smoked, regular and silken soft and silken firm. For desserts I tend to use the silken varieties. Silken tofu is bought in a 'tetrapack' and will keep for a few months without refrigeration. It should have a sell-by date on its top and once opened it is best used within a couple of days and kept in the refrigerator. I tend to liquidize the tofu before I use it for desserts as more often than not I use it to replace cream, and therefore need a smooth mixture. Silken soft, as the name suggests, is not as firm as silken firm and I use the former more for sauces and the latter for cheesecakes. They can be easily interchanged if you find you can't get hold of one variety.

Carob

Carob is in fact a legume and a member of the locust family (the plant, that is – not the insect). It has been used for thousands of years as a good source of nutrients. Many regard carob as an excellent substitute for chocolate as you can't tell the difference between them. Unlike chocolate, carob does not contain any caffeine, and doesn't require sweetening with sugar as it is naturally sweet.

You can buy carob in a powder form or in bars like chocolate and you can directly interchange carob for chocolate in any recipe. At the moment carob can usually be bought only in health shops – but it is becoming increasingly available. You can even buy carob 'chocolates' in elegant presentation boxes at Christmastime.

Flour

I use wholemeal flour in my cooking because it is better for your health and because I prefer the taste to its white counterpart. You can buy either 100 per cent or 85 per cent wholemeal flour. The former contains all the bran and germ of the wheat whereas the latter, as the name suggests, contains 85 per cent. It's the germ and the bran that are processed out of the refined white flours and along with them go the B and E vitamins. Wholemeal flour not only contains these vital vitamins but also more fibre – of which we all need more.

Be careful of using self-raising flours because they are very high in sodium – that's the offending mineral in salt which we should cut down on. It's far better to buy plain flour for all of your cooking and add your own low-sodium baking powder. Wholemeal flour can be bought from health shops or quite readily from supermarkets.

Low-Sodium Baking Powder

At the moment you can only buy this from good, well-stocked healthshops - but it is worth searching out. This type of baking powder can be used freely without harming your health. It is particularly useful for people such as those suffering from high blood pressure who have to reduce drastically their sodium intake.

Setting Agents

There are quite a few setting agents available to us these days. The one that most people are familiar with is gelatin which is made from ground hoofs and horns. The most convenient way to buy it is in powder form and it is usually sold in 11 gram packets. Gelatin is very easy to use and retains its clear quality when mixed with other things. It's particularly useful for those fruits suspended in clear juices. You will find that 3 teaspoons of gelatin will set 1 pint of liquid. All you have to do is place about 4 tablespoons of boiling water into a container and sprinkle on the gelatin. Stir well until it dissolves. Leave to cool slightly and then add to the other ingredients you wish to set. You can buy gelatin easily from supermarkets and corner shops.

Agar-agar is another setting agent which is derived from seaweed and is, therefore, useful for vegetarians. You can buy agar-agar from most healthshops and it comes in powder or flake form. Again, it is quite easy to use and also retains its clear quality. To set 1 pint of liquid you require about 2 teaspoons of agar-agar. Simply sprinkle the agar-agar onto cold liquid and then bring it to the boil, stirring constantly until it dissolves.

Gelozone is yet another vegetarian setting agent which is made from guar gum, carrageen and locust bean gum. It's simple to use but can go cloudy when mixed with other ingredients. As long as the end result doesn't need to be clear, the gelozone is an excellent choice of setting agent and is very useful in cheesecakes and mousses. The thing to remember about gelozone is that you must not bring it to the boil because it destroys its setting quality. To set 1 pint merely sprinkle 2 teaspoons onto some liquid and stir continuously. Heat until the mixture begins to steam.

Agar-agar and gelozone are available from good healthshops.

Low Fat Soft Cheese

There are quite a few low fat soft cheeses about now and they are easily available from supermarkets and corner shops. They taste every bit as rich as the full fat variety but are far healthier to eat. I always have some in my refrigerator. You can buy softer low fat soft cheeses in the form of *fromage frais* and quark. Both are made from skimmed milk and are much lower in fat, cholesterol and calories than their high-fat counterparts. Whilst full fat soft cheese contains around 440 calories per 100 grams, the 1 per cent variety of *fromage frais* contains a mere 100 calories, and quark only 70! Quite a difference isn't there? *Fromage frais* comes in two types: 1 per cent fat and 8 per cent fat. I tend to use the 1 per cent variety as it is healthier, but the 8 per cent fat *fromage frais* is still better than using cream. So if you prefer a creamier, richer taste then try the 8 per cent for a while before moving on the 1 per cent.

Quark is the German equivalent of *fromage frais* and is available in most supermarkets and healthshops.

Firmer low fat soft cheeses can be obtained from many cheese counters in large supermarkets and in pre-packaged 150 gram containers on the shelves. Cottage cheese and ricotta cheese are also useful low fat cheeses.

Low Fat Natural Yoghurt

Don't be tempted to use fruit-flavoured yoghurts as they contain added sugar. It is always far better to use low fat natural yoghurt with added fresh or dried fruit. If you like it a little sweeter then add a tiny drop of honey. Nothing else is required. Low fat natural yoghurt is an extremely useful alternative to cream as it contains less fat and only 52 calories per 100 grams. You can buy low fat natural yoghurt from supermarkets and healthshops. Different makes do have very different tastes and textures so it's better to shop around until you find your particular favourite.

Another useful cream alternative is Greek yoghurt. It is richer, containing about 8 per cent fat and therefore more calories – 135 per 100 grams. Still, Greek yoghurt is far healthier than cream. It is called Greek strained yoghurt (the whey is strained off the yoghurt to make it richer and creamier) and is available from most supermarkets and healthshops.

Milk

You will find that I always use either skimmed milk or soya milk in my recipes. This is because full cream milk has a high saturated fat content and contains much more cholesterol than skimmed or soya. The nutritional value of skimmed milk is virtually as good as full cream milk although there is a slight loss of the vitamins A, D and E, which are skimmed off along with the cream. Skimmed milk can be bought from supermarkets and corner shops. You can even have it delivered by your milkman!

Soya milk is useful in cooking because it has a rich and creamy flavour, without the fat and cholesterol. It's an excellent choice for sauces and creamy puddings. You can purchase it in bottles, cans, packets and in a dried form. Most larger supermarkets now carry a good stock of soya milk in either a sugar-free or sugar-added form. As soya milk contains less calcium, vitamin A and phosphorus than cow's milk, it is often fortified.

Both skimmed milk and soya milk contain approximately half the calories of full cream milk – 33 calories per 100 grams rather than 65. So it is well worth making the change – you really cannot notice the difference in sweets made with the lower calorie milk.

Fats

Just look at all the butters and margarines we can choose from today. No wonder we are confused. And, just when we thought we had the 'healthy' ones sorted out, low fat spreads made their appearance and confused the whole issue yet again.

By now most people are aware that butter is not good for our health because of its very high content of saturated fat, cholesterol and calories. So switching to margarines instead is an obvious move. But which one? In fact, some magarines are just as high in saturated fat, cholesterol and calories as butter. The best thing to do is to read the label carefully and choose a margarine which is high in polyunsaturates. This is the type of fat that can act in reducing cholesterol levels in the blood. By making the switch to polyunsaturated margarines you are reducing both the saturated fat as well as the cholesterol content of your diet. The calorific value however remains the same – at around 740 calories per 100 grams.

Most margarines, even those high in polyunsaturates, have gone through a process known as 'hydrogenation'. Hydrogen gas is pumped through the margarine in order to make it solid at room temperature. Let's fact it – we wouldn't want to buy a margarine that had the same consistency as oil, would we? The only problem with the hydrogenation process is that it converts polyunsaturated fatty acids into saturated acids. So when you read that some of the oils have been 'hydrogenated' in your tub of margarine read that as saturated fat.

At the moment there are only approximately three margarines which aren't hydrogenated and they are available from most good healthshops. The major problem is that hydrogenation is the cheapest way to make margarine as we like it – spreadable. Therefore, the unhydrogenated brands are relatively more expensive and more difficult to obtain.

And, what about all these low fat spreads that have emerged recently? Incidently, they are called a spread instead of margarine because, by law, a margarine has to contain over 80 per cent fat. Low fat spreads contain approximately 40 per cent fat. The calorific content of low fat spreads is, therefore, much less than that found in butter or margarine – 390 calories per 100 grams as opposed to 740. So low fat spreads appeal on two counts – a low level of fat and far fewer calories.

However, it's the type of fat as well as the amount that's important. While we should all aim to cut the amount of fat we consume, it's important to restrict saturated fat in favour of polyunsaturated. Once again, read the label and look for a spread high in polyunsaturates. Unfortunately, at the time of writing, there isn't one that is unhydrogenated, but we can expect something to appear on the market in the near future.

One thing to remember is that you are restricted by the number of things for which you can use low fat spreads. Because they have a high water content, once they are heated, the water and fats can separate, making them unsuitable for cooking in general.

At the end of the day you pay your money and take your choice. But just to sum up – it's important to reduce the total amount of fat you eat and also minimize saturated fat in favour of polyunsaturated. The benefits are countless.

Oils

The same theory behind the use of fats applies to oils – you should reduce not only the overall amount you consume but also the amount of saturated fat you use in favour of polyunsaturated. You do have quite a few to choose from and these include safflower oil, sunflower oil, sesame oil and soya oil. Try to avoid blended oils – even vegetable – as they use palm oil and coconut oil which are very high in saturated fatty acids.

It is also better to use cold pressed oils as they retain more nutrients than the more processed oils. Supermarkets stock quite a wide range of oils and so do healthshops.

Sweeteners

You will find that my recipes, in the main, do not contain any sugar at all. Some recipes, such as 'Sweetheart' do require a little to make the dish work. Sugar gives us nothing but empty calories – no nutrients whatsoever. And, contrary to popular belief, brown sugar is just as bad as white for your health. The difference in nutrient content is negligible. In fact a lot of brown sugars are white and merely coloured with caramel.

There are an abundance of things that you can use to replace the sugar in a recipe. With desserts that are particularly fruity I like to use fruit juices to sweeten the dish. Apple juice is especially good as it is one of the sweetest–tasting juices and yet it hasn't got a very strong flavour. Therefore, you can enhance the dish rather than overpower it. I also use orange juice quite a bit and I have found that it's wonderful combined with mangoes and even figs. You do need to remember to reduce the amount of liquid in 'ordinary' recipes, if you replace the sugar with a fruit juice, as you are automatically increasing the liquid content.

Concentrated fruit juices, available from healthshops, are quite useful as well. They have an extremely strong flavour and are quite thick. You can buy them in a variety of flavours such as apple and strawberry, and apple and pear. You don't need to use as much of a concentrated juice as you would a regular fruit juice. A little bit placed in a pan with some fresh fruit is wonderful for as you gently heat it, the juices mingle and the sweetness from the juice is absorbed. It tastes so much better than the traditional sugar-laden version.

Using fruit juices, regular and concentrated, is far better for you than using sugar as you not only reduce the calories and obtain a better flavour, but you also derive important nutrients from the juices. And they do not have the 'empty' calories of sugar.

Honey can also be used to replace sugar. It is particularly useful because it is sweeter than sugar and contains fewer calories because of its water content. So for the same sweetness, honey supplies less empty energy. I find that I need less than half the amount of honey as I would sugar in a recipe. The two main sweeteners in honey are fructose and glucose and, although sweeter than sucrose, they don't disrupt the blood sugar levels in the same way as sucrose does. However, they are still sugars and should be used in moderation. Honey does contain more nutrients than sugar but they are minimal to the point of insignificance.

Certain herbs are very useful for adding sweetness to a dessert. Sweet cicely and angelica – both fresh herbs – are a real asset to the kitchen. And you can grow them quite easily in your windowbox or garden. Angelica does, however, grow quite tall and soon outgrows a windowbox. With angelica it is the stem that you use – the leaves can be quite bitter. All you do is chop them up and add them to your dish instead of sugar. You use the leaves of sweet cicely: just chop them up and add to fruit crumbles and pies at your discretion.

Spices also add sweetness to desserts. Cinnamon is especially nice as it provides a mellow spicy flavour as well as a touch of sweetness to any dish.

Fruit

Fresh and dried fruits are wonderful – adding both flavour and texture to desserts. They are also useful for adding sweetness – especially dried fruits and bananas. The variety of fruits now available gives us an abundance from which to choose and with which to experiment.

Different types of fruit provide various nutrients and amounts of fibre. Generally speaking, fruits which contain seeds that you eat, such as raspberries, blackberries and passion fruit, have a higher fibre content than fruits such as melons and peaches. So fruits with tough skins and seeds that you eat are higher in fibre than tender fleshy fruits.

Fruits with yellow flesh, such as peaches, nectarines, yellow melons and apricots are the best fruit sources of vitamin A. Strawberries, blackcurrants and citrus fruits are excellent sources of vitamin C. In fact, one 100 gram portion of stewed blackcurrants provides over five times the daily recommended amount of vitamin C.

Fresh fruits are between 80–90 per cent water and therefore contain few calories – which makes them extremely useful as the base for many a dessert. You must always wash fruit very well – give them a really good scrub. With fruits that have a porous skin, such as peaches and apricots, peel them prior to use. Additives are allowed on the skin of fruits which is why some very shiny apples look as though they have been waxed – they probably have. Washing with soapy water will remove some of these additives but on fruits with a porous skin, more of the spray is absorbed and thus they are better peeled.

Organically grown fruit is making an appearance in some areas of the country and it is well worth buying it whenever you can. However, the supply is not great and the variety not too vast.

Dried fruits are a rich source of protein and minerals – not to mention fibre. They contain iron, calcium, vitamins A and C, and many of the B vitamins. The best way to dry fruit is to lay it out in the strong sunlight. More modern methods, however, include placing the fruit in sulphur houses. The highly poisonous gas of sulphur dioxide fumigates the fruit – this allows the colour of fruit, such as apricots, to be retained and the fruit to be dehydrated. Raisins and sultanas are dipped into a solution of potassium carbonate before being dried. And, if that isn't enough, fruit is very often sprayed with a mineral oil, such as liquid paraffin, to make the fruit look shiny, plump and more appealing to the customer.

Careful washing in very hot water can remove some of these additives but it is far better to buy naturally dried fruit that hasn't been treated with chemicals. Most healthshops stock dried fruits which are guaranteed not to have been sprayed, dipped and sulphurated. They may not look as nice when you buy them, but you can't tell the difference once they are contained within a dessert.

Dried fruit should be kept in an air-tight container. Under those circumstances it will keep for up to one year. You can also very successfully freeze all dried fruit.

Tinned fruit is a popular purchase for people, especially when fruit is expensive during the winter months. Do avoid buying canned fruit that has a sugar syrup with the fruit. Not only are the calories increased substantially but it also doesn't do your health any good. There are an increasing number of manufacturers now providing canned fruit in its own juice or with fruit juice. This is far better for you – read the label to ensure that it does not contain any added sugar.

Coffee

I sometimes use coffee in a recipe – just to give it a little bite. I always use a decaffeinated coffee. However, it's a little more complicated than merely reading the label on the jar and looking for the word 'decaffeinated'. You need to make sure that the brand you buy is decaffeinated by the water method. If it isn't the coffee you buy could be worse for your health than the caffeine-laden brands. The reason is that the majority of decaffeinated coffees have undergone a chemical process to remove the offending caffeine. Residues of the chemicals used are present in the coffee and can often be more dangerous to you than the caffeine they removed! If in doubt, contact the manufacturer to ask them what process they used to remove the caffeine. Caffeine acts as a stimulant and is addictive so it really is better avoided if at all possible.

Oats

You will find that when I make a cheesecake base or a crumble oats are present more often than not in the recipe. There is a reason for this: oats are a very good source of soluble fibre. This kind of fibre acts like a sponge inside the body, absorbing harmful fats and toxins and passing them quickly through the body. This minimizes the chance of the fats and toxins being absorbed in our blood and body tissue, hence reducing the risk of various forms of cancer and cholesterol problems – that's got to be good news for everyone.

Filo or Strudel Pastry

You will find a whole chapter of my book, 'Filo Fantasies', devoted to this paper-thin pastry. Because it is very thin, just like tissue paper, it is quite low in calories and is, therefore, a useful addition to the kitchen store cupboard. You can buy filo from the larger supermarkets in frozen form or from delicatessens. Try to make sure that the shop you buy from has a rapid stock turnover as filo only keeps for a couple of months before it becomes unmanageable.

When you first buy filo pastry you will probably feel overwhelmed by all the tissue-thin leaves of pastry laid out before you – I know I was initially. However, you soon get used to its consistency and it is certainly worth that initial bit of effort to learn its various uses.

In every 100 grams of filo pastry there are only 275 calories and only 4.2 per cent fat. That, for pastry, is very good. Filo pastry is very versatile as it can be moulded into many different shapes.

Eggs

You'll find that egg yolks have been banished from this book. I do, however, use egg whites occasionally. The yolk of an egg is very high in both saturated fat and cholesterol. When I do use the whites, I make sure that I use fresh free-range eggs. Free-range eggs are becoming much more widely available and many supermarkets do stock them.

People are switching to free-range eggs not only for humanitarian reasons but also because of health factors. Battery hens are quite often given antibiotics and drugs, traces of which can be left in the eggs. The yolks are often 'yellowed' by colourings put in the hen's feed. So it is far better to use free-range – this kind of artificial stimulation is far less likely to occur because the hens remain healthy in a wholesome environment.

Chapter Three
A Word About the Recipes

Every single recipe in this book is good for your health for each of the desserts is very low in fat – especially saturated – low in sugar, relatively high in fibre, and nutritious. Each recipe has also been tried and tested – not only by me. You will notice that each of the recipes has been marked either 'Richard Proof' or 'Not Richard Proof'. Yes, you've guessed it. My husband Richard has attempted to make every single recipe. And I assure you that is no easy task for Richard.

Richard is not a cook – by any stretch of the imagination. He can just about manage to make toasted sandwiches and steam some vegetables, that's his limit. I must admit that I didn't think Richard would have successfully completed the number of recipes he did and there were only one or two real disasters in the kitchen.

So if the recipe is 'Richard Proofed', believe me, you can make it without any difficulty whatsoever. The recipes where Richard did experience a slight problem contain a brief explanation of what went wrong. This may give you an idea of how to avoid any possible mishap. I found that while writing my cookery books it was easy to take too much for granted. For example, in one recipe I said 'cream together the margarine and honey'. To Richard this merely meant gently combining the ingredients together instead of beating them really well. I assumed that he would know what the term 'cream together' actually meant, but he didn't. And, when you think about it, why on earth should he know? Needless to say that recipe was a disaster. The mixture turned out to be a heavy, flat doorstop instead of light and fluffy.

Each of the recipes gives you the number of servings and the calories contained in the serving. I also indicate whether or not the dessert can be frozen.

To give you a good idea of the conversion process involved in substituting ingredients, I give a couple of 'Swap Shop' recipes in each chapter. This is particularly useful as it gives you an idea of how to convert your own favourite recipes into healthy alternatives.

You will notice that the ingredients in each recipe are given in both imperial and metric weights – please use one or the other, *not both*, when you're making one of the desserts. You may also find the following conversion tables quite useful. I know that we are all supposed to be metricated but I, for one, remain unconverted. My mind still, very stubbornly, thinks in terms of the old pounds and ounces.

Measurement Equivalents			
Grams (g)	Ounces (oz)	Millilitres (ml)	Fluid Ounces (fl. oz)
25	1	25	1
40	$1^1/_2$	50	2
50	2	75	3
60	$2^1/_2$	125	4
75	3	150	5 ($^1/_4$ pint)
100	4	175	6
125	4	200	7
150	5	225	8
175	6	250	10 ($^1/_2$ pint)
200	7	275	10 ($^1/_2$ pint)
225	8	300	11
250	9	350	12
275	10	375	13
300	11	400	15 ($^3/_4$ pint)
350	12	425	16 ($^3/_4$ pint)
375	13	450	17
400	14	475	18
425	15	500	20 (1 pint)
450	16	550	20 (1 pint)
475	17	575	30
500	18	850	35
700	24	1000	40
1000	2 pounds	1.2 litres	

No doubt you will notice that for some of the imperial weights and measures given in the tables there are two possible metric equivalents. No wonder we are confused. For some of the recipes I have used one equivalent and for other recipes I have chosen the other equivalent. It all depends on what each particular recipe calls for.

The tablespoons and teaspoons used in my recipes are the standard sizes of 15ml and 5ml respectively, and should be level, not heaped.

Centimetres to inches	
Centimetres	Inches
6mm	$^1/_4$in
1cm	$^1/_2$in
2.5cm	1in
5cm	2in
7.5cm	3in
10cm	4in
12.5cm	5in
15cm	6in
18cm	7in
20cm	8in
23cm	9in
25cm	10in
28cm	11in
30cm	12in

Oven Temperatures			
Temperature	*Centrigrade (C)*	*Fahrenheit (F)*	*Gas Mark (GM)*
	70	150	
	80	175	
	100	200	
VERY COOL	110	225	$1/_4$
	120	250	$1/_2$
	140	275	1
COOL	150	300	2
WARM	160	325	3
	180	350	4
FAIRLY HOT	190	375	5
	200	400	6
	220	425	7
HOT	230	450	8
VERY HOT	240	475	9
	260	500	9

Just a quick word on oven temperatures. Ovens can vary enormously and you will probably know whether yours runs hotter or cooler than it should. My Mum's oven is a very hot one whilst mine tends to be on the cooler side. The temperatures given in the recipes should therefore be used only as a guide. If you know your oven to be hot then reduce the temperature accordingly. The reverse is also true if your oven is cooler.

North American Measurement Equivalents		
1pint/575ml	water	$2^1/_4$ cups
1oz /25g	margarine	2 tbsp
1oz /25g	flour	2 tbsp
1oz /25g	chopped seeds	2 tbsp
1oz /25g	grated cheese	4 tbsp
1lb /450g	breadcrumbs	8 cups
1lb /450g	rice (uncooked)	2 cups
1lb /450g	wholemeal flour	4 cups
1lb /450g	mashed potato	2 cups
1lb /450g	small beans	2 cups
1lb /450g	large beans	3 cups
1lb /450g	ground seeds	4 cups
1lb /450g	cottage cheese	2 cups
1lb /450g	soft cheese	2 cups

Chapter Four
Playing the Fool

Mousses and fools are beautifully light and creamy desserts which are perfect to conclude a rather filling meal. As we would say in Yorkshire, they don't make you feel 'pogged'. For those of you who are not accustomed to our sayings, 'pogged' means over-full with food. Mousses and fools are extremely quick and easy to make and look most attractive when piled into long stemmed glasses with a sprig of mint to garnish.

Hollowed out fruits, such as oranges, lemons, kiwi etc, can be used to show off your mousses to great effect. You can present them so attractively that any dinner party guests would be impressed by their appearance and taste.

These desserts can be extremely low in calories, fat and cholesterol if you make certain changes to the recipes. The cream, eggs and sugar of the traditional mousse or fool can all be very easily replaced by other, healthier, ingredients. Tofu provides a very low-calorie base for mousses and fools and yet tastes so rich and creamy that you would swear you were eating double cream. Many fruits will naturally sweeten the desserts without the need to add sugar to the recipe. Bananas are particularly wonderful as you merely whip them up with the tofu in a liquidizer and there you have it – a sweet-tasting cream. It really couldn't be easier. And, once you get into the habit of swapping ingredients around, it does become second nature and you will begin to do it without even having to think about it.

To enjoy mousses and fools throughout the year I freeze fresh fruit in a pureed form and use this to give me a basis for flavour. This method works very well. If you freeze fruit whole there is a tendency for too much water to be retained in the fruit, which can make the mousses a little watery. You don't have to rely on fresh fruits either. You can very successfully use dried fruits which will give the dessert the benefit of additional fibre content. You can also layer the mousses and fools with other high-fibre ingredients such as oats, oat bran, seeds and fruit. As well as adding interest to the dessert in both looks and texture you are also increasing nutrition. And that can't be a bad thing, can it? For very subtle and delicate desserts why not try using herbs either on their own or mixed with fruit. They really do give another dimension to the taste. Mint works particularly well and is loved by everyone. Thyme is another herb which is useful and gives a distinctive flavour to these light desserts. The combinations can go on and on forever – and it's all great fun.

The success of fools and mousses really lies in adequately whisking the egg whites to get as much air in them as possible. The other crucial factor is being able to maintain that air whilst folding the egg whites into the remaining ingredients.

Richard does have problems in this respect, I must admit. He is like a bull in a china shop. He literally beats them in instead of carefully folding them. You must be 'light of hand' when performing this part of the technique. Richard now stands there with the bowl in front of him and a look of intense concentration on his face as he repeats the words 'figure of eight, light of hand' and carefully mixes. He has become quite the little expert!

Magic Carpet

A mousse is loved by children and adults alike and this one is as light as air. In fact, one of our guests said it made her feel as light as if she were floating on a cloud!

Ingredients: Imperial/Metric

4oz/100g	dried, pitted prunes
1	lemon (zest)
2tsp	gelatin
3tbsp	fresh lemon juice
1tbsp	honey
7fl oz/200ml	*fromage frais*
2	egg whites

Richard Proof

Serves:	4
Calories:	55
Soaking Time:	Overnight
Preparation Time:	20 minutes
Cooking Time:	15 minutes
Chilling Time:	45 minutes

Garnish:

1   lemon for lemon twists
2   prunes, chopped

Method:

1   Soak the prunes in cold water overnight.
2   Simmer the prunes and lemon zest in a covered pan for about 15 minutes, with just enough water to cover.
3   Soak the gelatin in a small basin with the lemon juice.
4   Drain the prunes, reserving 150ml of the cooking liquid.
5   While they are still hot, place the prunes in a blender with the reserved juice, gelatin and honey. Blend until smooth and turn into a bowl to cool.
6   Whisk the egg white until stiff.
7   As the prune mixture begins to set, carefully fold in the *fromage frais* and egg white.
8   Spoon the mousse into a glass serving dish and chill in the refrigerator until set.
9   Garnish with the chopped prunes and lemon twists.

Swap Shop Recipe
Pucker Up

Have you noticed that when you eat rhubarb your mouth puckers? Well, its because of the tannins in the fruit which react with the lining of your mouth. These spare tannins can also cause constipation. This tasty and delicious dessert will only cause delight!

Richard Proof   *Serves*: 6
Preparation Time: 20 minutes   *Cooking Time*: 10 minutes

Traditional version

Healthier version

Calories: 293

Calories: 62

Ingredients: Imperial/Metric		**Ingredients:** Imperial/Metric	
1	orange (zest and juice)	1	orange (zest and juice)
1³/₄lb/900g	rhubarb	1³/₄lb/900g	rhubarb
3fl oz/75ml	red fruit jam	3oz/75ml	sugar-free red fruit jam
4oz/125g	caster sugar	1tbsp	honey
10fl oz/250ml	double cream	10fl oz/250ml	firm silken tofu, liquidized

Garnish:
orange zest

Garnish:
orange zest

Method:
Put the rhubarb into a saucepan with the fresh orange juice, sugar-free jam and honey.
Cover and simmer gently until the rhubarb is soft and pulpy.
Cool slightly and purée in a blender. Leave to cool.
Add the orange zest and gently fold in the tofu.
Spoon into six individual glass dishes and garnish with the orange twists.

TIP BOX
Never cook rhubarb in aluminium pans and don't use aluminium utensils. The acid in the rhubarb eats away at the aluminium and it seeps into the juices.

Bells of St Clements

This mousse has the most wonderful aroma you can imagine – just like orange blossom on a hot, sunny day.

Ingredients: Imperial/Metric

10fl oz/250ml	low fat natural yoghurt
6fl oz/175ml	fresh orange juice
1	orange (zest)
2tsp	orange flower water
2	egg whites
½oz/11g	gelatin

Richard Proof

Serves:	6
Calories:	34
Preparation Time:	5 minutes
Chilling Time:	4 hours

Garnish:

8 orange wings

Method:

1 Dissolve the gelatin in two tablespoons of boiling water.
2 Whisk the yoghurt, orange juice and gelatin together.
3 Add the orange zest and orange flower water.
4 Whisk the egg whites until stiff and fold into the mixture.
5 Pour the mixture into a freezer container and place in the freezer until frozen.
6 Spoon into individual glasses and garnish with the orange wings.

TIP BOX

To make lemon, lime or orange wings, simply work from the top towards the base of the unpeeled fruit, making 2 small diagonal cuts in the centre. Angle the knife so that you obtain a wedge. Remove the wedge and keep for later. Cut three more wedges out of the fruit following the same angle as the first – each wedge will be larger than the previous one. Repeat this process four times, working round the fruit. You should finish with four sets of four wedges, resembling wings.

St John's Bread

Edible pods and beans are often referred to as St John's Bread and that term relates back to John the Baptist – remember that he lived on locusts and wild honey in the wilderness. It was the locust bean he ate, not the insect as many think. The combination of carob and banana works very well, giving the dessert a natural sweetness. St John's Bread is the richest of desserts with a creamy texture and strong chocolatey flavour. A beautiful way to conclude any meal!

Ingredients: Imperial/Metric

4oz/100g	carob bar, sugar free
4fl oz/125ml	firm tofu
4fl oz/125ml	*fromage frais*
1	large, ripe banana

Richard Proof
Serves: 6
Calories: 80
Preparation Time: 15 minutes

Garnish:
6   carob curls

Method:
1   Break the carob bar into small pieces and place in a bowl over a pan of hot water. Stir until melted. Leave to cool slightly.
2   Place the tofu in a liquidizer with 1 tablespoon of the *fromage frais* and the banana. Blend until smooth. Fold in the remaining *fromage frais*.
3   Mix together the carob and tofu mixture and spoon into 6 individual glasses.
4   Garnish with the carob curls.

TIP BOX
Carob is a natural alternative to chocolate. Not only does it have less fat and fewer calories but it is naturally sweet and caffeine free.

29

Passion

Passion fruit has a strong aroma and a distinctive flavour which makes this dessert an absolute pleasure to the senses. The crunchy seeds give this fool a lovely texture.

Ingredients: Imperial/Metric

4	passion fruit
1	banana
1	lemon (zest and juice)
7fl oz/200ml	*fromage frais*

Richard Proof
Serves: 4
Calories: 64
Preparation Time: 5 minutes

Garnish:
4 nasturtium flowers

Method:
1 Cut the passion fruit in half and scoop out the seedy centre.
2 Mash the passion fruit to a smooth consistency.
3 Mash the banana and lemon juice together.
4 Add the lemon zest and passion fruit.
5 Fold in the *fromage frais*, chill for two hours and pile into glasses.
6 Garnish with the nasturtium flowers.

Limey

Lime juice was commonly given to British seamen in the mid-nineteenth century and that's how they got the nickname 'limey'. An unusual combination of ingredients – I know – but this mousse works extremely well.

Ingredients: Imperial/Metric

5oz/150g	ripe greengages
1	lime (zest and juice)
10fl oz/250ml	soft silken tofu
10fl oz/250ml	*fromage frais*

Richard Proof
Serves: 4
Calories: 109
Preparation Time: 10 minutes

Garnish:
12 lime wings
2tsp lime zest

Method:
1 Wash and stone the greengages and place them in a liquidizer with the tofu. Blend until smooth.
2 Gradually stir in the lime juice and zest.
3 Carefully fold in the *fromage frais*.
4 Spoon into long-stemmed glasses and garnish with the lime wings and zest.

Swap Shop Recipe
Greensleeves

This mousse is a traditional favourite and even nicer with healthier ingredients. Look at the difference in calories!

Richard Proof   *Serves*: 6   *Preparation Time*: 15 minutes
Cooking Time: 10 minutes   *Chilling Time*: 10 minutes

Traditional version

Calories: 247

Healthier version

Calories: 66

Ingredients: Imperial/Metric		**Ingredients:** Imperial/Metric	
1¹/₂lb/700g	cooking apples	1¹/₂lb/700g	cooking apples
4oz/125g	caster sugar	2tbsp	apple juice
2tbsp	water	2tbsp	water
4fl oz/125ml	double cream	4fl oz/125ml	low fat natural yoghurt
2	egg whites	2	egg whites
1tbsp	muscavado sugar	1tbsp	honey

Garnish:		**Garnish:**	
1fl oz/25ml	double cream	1fl oz/25ml	*fromage frais*
6	mint sprigs	6	mint sprigs

Method:
Slice the apples into a pan and add the apple juice, water and mint. Cover and simmer for 10 minutes.
Remove the mint. Blend in a liquidizer until smooth. Leave to cool and then fold in the yoghurt.
Whisk the egg whites until stiff and fold into the apple mixture.
Spoon into individual glasses and garnish with the *fromage frais* and mint.

The Blushing Bride

This dessert is deceptively healthy and would satisfy the most ardent 'traditional' eater. The beauty of it is that it's so easy and quick to make that you can literally whip it up to order. Piled into tall elegant glasses 'Blushing Bride' looks sophisticated and classy.

Richard Proof
Serves: 4
Calories: 45
Preparation Time: 5 minutes
Chilling Time: 2 hours

Ingredients: Imperial/Metric	
1pt/500ml	*fromage frais*
8oz/225g	strawberries

Garnish:

4   strawberries

Method:

1   Place 2 tablespoons of the *fromage frais* in a liquidizer with the
strawberries. Blend until smooth.

2   Carefully fold the remaining *fromage frais* into the strawberry mixture.

3   Chill for 2 hours.

4   Spoon into 4 tall-stemmed glasses and garnish with strawberry fans.

> **TIP BOX**
> Rinse strawberries under cool running water just before you want to use them. Then pull off their heads. If you hull strawberries before rinsing them you will dilute their flavour, as water gets into the fruit.

Spice of Life

The addition of ginger to this dessert gives it a nice 'bite', which is very refreshing in a mousse. I love ginger anyway, so it has got to be a favourite of mine!

Ingredients: Imperial/Metric

4oz/125g	quark
$\frac{1}{2}$tsp	ground ginger
2tbsp	sugar-free marmalade
1	orange (zest)
5fl oz/150ml	firm silken tofu

Richard Proof

Serves:	4
Calories:	70
Preparation Time:	5 minutes

Garnish:

4   pieces of stem ginger

4   lavender heads

Method:

1   Mix together the quark, ground ginger, marmalade and orange zest.

2   Liquidize the tofu until smooth. Gently fold into the cheese mixture.

3   Spoon into four glasses and garnish with the stem ginger and lavender heads.

Chaffey

In California the Chaffey brothers were famed for their apricots and, in the 1880s, started the dried fruit industry in Australia. This is one of my favourite syllabubs because I love the tartness of the apricots when they are combined with the creamy *fromage frais*.

Ingredients: Imperial/Metric

3oz/75g	dried apricots
7fl oz/200ml	apple juice
3	egg whites
7fl oz/200ml	*fromage frais*

Richard Proof
Serves: 6
Calories: 36
Soaking Time: Overnight
Preparation Time: 10 minutes
Cooking Time: 5 minutes

Garnish:
3 dried apricots
6 fresh mint sprigs

Method:
1 Wash the apricots well and soak in the apple juice overnight.
2 Bring the apricots and apple juice to a boil and simmer for about 5 minutes. Leave to cool.
3 Place the apricot mixture in a liquidizer and blend until smooth. Fold into the *fromage frais*.
4 Whisk the egg whites until stiff and carefully fold into the apricot mixture.
5 Spoon into serving dishes and garnish each with half a dried apricot and a mint sprig.

> **TIP BOX**
> When you buy dried apricots, choose the brownish looking ones, as the bright orange ones, although more attractive, have been sulphurated. If in doubt, ask for unsulphurated dried apricots.

Punch and Judy

It's such a shame that delicious damsons come and go so quickly – one minute market stalls are full of them and the next minute there isn't a solitary one to be found. They are a beautiful rich red in colour and they have a unique taste. Combined with the creamy egg whites and tart yoghurt, the damsons make this mousse a 'taste sensation'.

Ingredients: Imperial/Metric

1lb/450g	damsons
1tbsp	honey
3	egg whites
11fl oz/300ml	low fat natural yoghurt
1tbsp	Norfolk Punch

Richard Proof
Serves: 8
Calories: 56
Preparation Time: 15 minutes
Cooking Time: 5 minutes

Garnish:
6 lemon wings

Method:

1 Gently cook the damsons and honey until the damsons are soft. Remove the stones.
2 Stir in the Norfolk Punch.
3 Mix together the damson mixture and yoghurt.
4 Whisk the egg whites until stiff and fold into the damson mixture.
5 Pile into eight glasses and garnish with lemon wings.

Metchnikoff

The Russian scientist Metchnikoff was the first person to claim the health-giving properties of yoghurt. This is one of Richard's favourite desserts. He likes the tang of the lemon and the sweetness of the peach. It's very quick and easy to make and tastes quite rich.

Ingredients: Imperial/Metric

10fl oz/250ml	low fat natural yoghurt
1tbsp	honey
1	lemon (zest and juice)
2	egg whites
1	peach, peeled and chopped

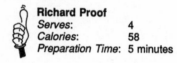

Richard Proof
Serves: 4
Calories: 58
Preparation Time: 5 minutes

Garnish:
lemon zest

Method:

1 Mix together the yoghurt, honey, peach, lemon zest and juice.
2 Whisk the egg whites until stiff and gently fold into the mixture.
3 Spoon into four glasses and garnish with the lemon zest.

TIP BOX

One day I saw a Greek friend of mine (whose family grew peaches) peeling peaches. I couldn't understand this as I love the skins – she maintained that she would never eat a peach with its skin on because of all the chemicals sprayed onto it. Because they have a furry skin they absorb more and it's impossible to get rid of all the chemicals by washing. Since then, I always boil my peaches and apricots for a few moments and then peel off their skins.

Twenty-two Carat

Carob seeds were actually used as a form of currency in the Middle East and from this we derive the term 'carat', used by jewellers today.

Richard loves this one – it's very rich and chocolatey. The texture of the mousse is smooth and silky and it tastes as though it should be very bad for your health and figure – but of course, it isn't!

Ingredients: Imperial/Metric

3oz/75g	carob bar, sugar-free
¹/₂fl oz/15ml	decaffeinated instant coffee
4	egg whites
1tbsp	honey

Not Richard Proof
Richard managed to get water into the carob mixture which made it lumpy instead of smooth. He tried again with new ingredients and managed it!

Serves: 4
Calories: 72
Preparation Time: 15 minutes

Garnish:

4	carob fans
1tbsp	grated carob

Method:
1. Break the carob into small pieces and place in a small bowl with the coffee and honey.
2. Place the bowl over a pan of hot water and stir until the carob has melted and the mixture is smooth and silky.
3. Whisk the egg whites until stiff and carefully fold into the carob mixture. Try not to stir out the air from the whisked egg whites. Gentle is the name of the game here.
4. Once all the egg white is folded in and cannot be seen, you can spoon the mixture into individual glasses.
5. Garnish each with a carob fan and a little grated chocolate.

TIP BOX

Carob fans are a delightful way to garnish any dessert and can be made in any shape or size. Simply melt about 3oz/75g of carob in a bowl over a pan of hot (not boiling) water. When melted, use a spoon or a narrow-nozzled piping bag to create a fan-shaped pattern on a sheet of greaseproof paper. Let cool and peel from the paper. The fans can be kept for months in an air-tight container. Why not try Christmas trees for the Christmas season or something for a birthday party?

Pink Panther

This is a beautifully light and fluffy dessert which is ideal after a big meal. Any other soft fruits can be used instead of bilberries for a change – redcurrants are particularly nice. If you like a smooth mixture you can strain the fruit and just retain the juice. I personally like whole bilberries suspended in the 'fluff' and, of course, more fibre is retained.

Ingredients: Imperial/Metric

14oz/400g	bilberries
1tbsp	apple juice
2tsp	Gelozone
3	egg whites

Garnish:
lemon and orange zest

Not Richard Proof
Richard left the 'fluff' too long before folding in the egg whites. The result was quite lumpy.

Serves:	6
Calories:	40
Preparation Time:	15 minutes
Chilling Time:	2 hours

Method:

1 Place the bilberries and juice in a pan and sprinkle on the Gelozone. Mix in quickly with a fork. Cook gently until the juice just begins to run and steam. Do not allow to boil.
2 Leave the mixture to cool.
3 When the mixture begins to set, gently fold in the egg white.
4 Spoon into individual glasses, or moulds, and leave to set in the refrigerator.
5 Rinse the outside of the glasses or moulds with hot water and turn out the bilberry fluff onto serving plates.
6 Garnish with the lemon and orange zest.

36

Swap Shop Recipe
Bramble

The profusion of fruits make this traditional dessert not only high in fibre, but also naturally sweet. The creaminess belies its fat and calorie content.

 Richard Proof   *Serves*: 10   *Preparation Time*: 30 minutes
Cooking Time: 10 minutes   *Chilling Time*: 4 hours

Traditional version

Healthier version

Calories: 396

Calories: 73

Ingredients: Imperial/Metric

4oz/125g	caster sugar
4oz/125g	blackcurrants
4oz/125g	redcurrants
7tsp	gelatin
4oz/125g	raspberries
3fl oz/75ml	orange squash
1fl oz/25ml	lemon juice
5fl oz/150ml	soured cream
12oz/350g	full fat soft cheese
7fl oz/200ml	double cream
2	eggs, separated

Ingredients: Imperial/Metric

2tbsp	honey
4oz/125g	blackcurrants
4oz/125g	redcurrants
7tsp	gelatin
4oz/125g	raspberries
1	orange (zest and juice)
1	lemon (zest and juice)
5fl oz/150ml	*fromage frais*
12oz/350g	low fat soft cheese
7fl oz/200ml	firm silken tofu, liquidized
2	egg whites

Method:

In a saucepan gently heat 1tbsp of honey with 100ml of water.

Top and tail the currants and add these to the water.

Cook until the fruit is just soft.

Meanwhile, in a small bowl sprinkle 2tsp of gelatin over 30ml of water and leave for a few moments.

Off the heat stir into the fruit until dissolved. Leave to cool.

Hull the raspberries and add to the fruit mixture. Pour into a $2^1/_4$pt/1.2 ltr ring mould and chill until set.

Place the 1tbsp of honey, *fromage frais*, low fat soft cheese, orange and lemon zest and juice into a liquidizer and blend until smooth.

Dissolve the remaining gelatin in 3tbsp of water in a small bowl over a pan of boiling water.

Add to the mixture in the liquidizer and blend for a moment.

Turn the mixture into a bowl. Gently fold in the tofu.

Whisk the egg whites until stiff and gently fold into the mixture.

Pour onto the ring mould and chill until set. Unmould and serve.

White Nun

The syllabub has a long English history and dates back to before the seventeenth century. It is usually made with cider and lots of double cream and thus, is quite high in fat, cholesterol and calories. My version uses healthier ingredients and yet looks and tastes just as nice. I love these in the height of summer when I can snatch five minutes of relaxation in the garden – lovely!

Ingredients: Imperial/Metric

4fl oz/125ml	firm silken tofu, liquidized
7fl oz/200ml	*fromage frais*
1	lemon (zest)
1fl oz/ 25ml	apple juice

Richard proof
Serves: 4
Calories: 50
Preparation Time 5 minutes
Chilling Time: 1 hour

Garnish:

4	lemon twists
4	fresh mint sprigs

Method:
1. Mix together the tofu and *fromage frais.*
2. Add the lemon zest.
3. Gradually stir in the apple juice and combine well.
4. Spoon into four tall, elegant glasses and chill for an hour.
5. Garnish with lemon twists and mint.

> **TIP BOX**
> To make lemon twists, simply wash the skin of a fresh lemon, slicing about $1/_2$ inch off one end. With a sharp knife, cut several slices of lemon – not more than $1/_4$ inch/6ml thick. Take each slice and make one cut from the centre of the lemon through the skin on one edge. With the cut edge facing you, simply twist one side of the lemon up, and the other down. This pretty twist can be set on any dish – sweet or savoury.

Apple Fromage

This is a very simple dessert to make and takes only a few minutes – perfect for a last minute effort. I make this quite a lot when apples are in abundance during the autumn months.

Ingredients: Imperial/Metric

14oz/400g	cooking apples
8fl oz/225ml	*fromage frais*

Richard proof
Serves: 4
Calories: 58
Preparation Time: 5 minutes

Garnish:

4   sprigs of fresh mint

Method:

1   Wash the apples in soapy water and then grate them into the *fromage frais*.

2   Mix well, making sure that the apples are coated fully with the *fromage frais* as this will prevent the apples from turning brown.

3   Pile the mixture onto individual serving plates and garnish with the mint.

TIP BOX

Apples are high in pectin which is a natural anti-diarrhoeal. According to old wives' tales, raw grated apple was given as a remedy for diarrhoea. In fact, purified pectin is an ingredient in most anti-diarrhoeals, such as kaolin, which you can buy at the chemist.

Taj Mahal

These days mango is readily available from supermarkets and market stalls. And although they seem quite an extravagant fruit, their flavour and perfume allow you to stretch them into quite a few servings. This mousse is particularly creamy and easy to make.

Ingredients: Imperial/Metric

1	mango, large and ripe
8fl oz/225ml	low fat natural yoghurt
1/2tsp	Gelozone
5fl oz/150ml	orange juice
4fl oz/125ml	*fromage frais*

Richard proof

Serves:	6
Calories:	50
Preparation Time:	10 minutes
Chilling Time:	3 hours

Garnish:

6   fresh mint sprigs

6   lavender heads

TIP BOX

Mangoes are an excellent source of vitamins A and C, if you eat them fresh and ripe.

Method:

1   Peel the mango, chop the flesh and liquidize it until smooth.

2   Add the yoghurt and blend.

3   Place the orange juice in a small pan and sprinkle on the Gelozone. Mix well with a fork. Heat gently until it begins to steam. Do not allow to boil. Leave to cool slightly.

4   Stir the orange juice into the yoghurt mixture and carefully stir in the *fromage frais*.

5   Spoon into six individual glasses and garnish with the mint and lavender.

High Balls

Prunes are a natural laxative, not because they are high in fibre, but because they contain a natural substance similar to biscodyl – the active ingredient in many laxatives and suppositories. This mousse is surprisingly light and fluffy – and honey and prunes are always a delicious combination.

Ingredients: Imperial/Metric

7oz/200g	prunes, pitted
5fl oz/150ml	low fat natural yoghurt
1tbsp	honey
10fl oz/250ml	*fromage frais*

Richard proof

Serves:	6
Calories:	71
Preparation Time:	10 minutes
Cooking Time:	10 minutes

Garnish:
6   sprigs of fresh mint
6   prunes, halved

Method:
1   Place the prunes in a pan with just enough water to cover and simmer for about 10 minutes. Leave to cool slightly.
2   Place the prunes in a liquidizer with their juice and blend until smooth. Leave to cool.
3   Mix together the yoghurt, honey and prunes.
4   Carefully fold in the *fromage frais* and spoon into glasses.
5   Garnish with the prune halves and mint sprigs.

TIP BOX
Buy prunes which are dull and crinkled rather than shiny as these have been coated with liquid paraffin.

Chapter Five
Feeling Fruity

If, like me, you have ordered a fresh fruit salad in a restaurant and ended up with a slice or two of banana, some chopped apple and, if you're lucky, a strawberry or two, then you could be forgiven for thinking of fruit as being dull and boring. I know from experience that a fairly local restaurant, a posh one at that, thinks that a fruit salad is exotic if it has banana in it!

It's such a shame that fresh fruit is dogged by such an undeservedly bad reputation. The variety of fresh fruit is marvellous. From all over the world we import fruit of every shape, size, colour and flavour. No longer the preserve of the specialist fruit shop, such exotic fruit as kiwi, passion, papaya and star are available from the supermarket shelves. The world's flavours are on our doorstep.

Many of us have experienced these fruits on our holidays abroad and have grown accustomed to them. The first time we ate fresh figs we were on an unspoilt Greek island called Syros. Some friendly Greeks picked some figs and presented them to us on a plate, complete with knife. I don't think that I have ever enjoyed fruit as much. Every Greek holiday since we have spent lots of time hunting down fig trees and raiding them – though not if they were in someone's garden! What a lovely way to spend a holiday. Whilst other tourists are bringing Greek souvenirs back to England, we load ourselves down with pounds and pounds of fresh figs, all carefully packed, and large tins of olive oil. What a sight we must look at the airport!

It's funny that fruit never quite taste the same as in their native country. Watermelons taste wonderful in hot Mediterranean countries but somehow seem to lack that special something if the temperature isn't a soaring 40°C, and you're not imbued with the odour of sun tan cream!

I adore all fresh fruit with the exception of just one – the Thai durian, whose taste strongly resembles the aroma of a tom cat. The problem with exotic fruits, as with anything that's unfamiliar to us, is that we're not quite sure what to do with them. Take the passion fruit as a case in point. This fruit looks so unpromising in its dark brown, wrinkled shell that it belies its real attraction. Once this ugly façade is cut open the most wonderful aroma floats out, filling the air with sweet perfume. The flesh and seeds can be scooped out and eaten with relish. They add a new dimension to any fruit-based dish.

Most supermarkets now provide leaflets which explain how unusual fruit can be prepared, giving serving suggestions.

It really is worth experimenting with the whole spectrum of fruit which is now readily available to us. After all, they have everything going for them. Not only are they extremely low in calories and fat and good sources of fibre and nutrients, but they also provide a stunning range of colour, taste and texture. And, on top of all this, most fruit doesn't require any cooking, which makes it quick and easy to prepare as well. In fact, its just what the doctor ordered!

Aaron's Rod

Almonds were mentioned in the Old Testament and are associated with one of the very first miracles – Aaron's rod was made to blossom and bear almonds. We have a couple of almond trees in our garden and they produce the most beautiful small white flowers in the spring – we haven't had any almonds yet but we live in hope. The almonds in this delicious fruit dish give it added crunch – and fibre. Naturally sweet and colourful, this dessert is a favourite in our home.

Ingredients: Imperial/Metric

1	pineapple
4	tangerines, washed
3oz/75g	black grapes, washed
4oz/125g	raspberries, washed
1tbsp	rosewater

Richard Proof

Serves:	6
Calories:	49
Preparation Time:	15 minutes
Marinating Time:	1 hour

Garnish:

4	variegated geranium flowers
$\frac{1}{2}$oz/11g	slivered almonds

Method:

1 Cut the pineapple in half lengthways – cutting right through the leafy crown. Remove the flesh and cut into chunks, discarding the central core. Put the pineapple 'shells' to one side.
2 Remove the zest from the tangerines with a zester and then peel them.
3 Cut the black grapes in half and remove the seeds.
4 Mix all the fruit together and stir in the rosewater. Leave to marinate for 1 hour.
5 Pile the fruit into the two pineapple halves, garnish with the geranium flowers and sprinkle with slivered almonds.

Mesopotamia

Cherries originated in the near East, in Mesopotamia, and were not imported into Europe until quite recently. This fruit does tend to be quite expensive and so I use them mixed with other, cheaper, fruit. The bright colours of this dish make it an attractive addition to any meal: it's particularly lovely in summer when the fruit is fresh.

Ingredients: Imperial/Metric

8oz/225g	cherries, washed
1	kiwi, washed
1	banana
4oz/100g	strawberries, washed

Richard Proof
Serves: 4
Calories: 62
Preparation Time: 10 minutes

Garnish:

4   lemon twists

Method:

1 Halve the cherries and remove the stones.
2 Slice the kiwi fruit quite thinly.
3 Slice the strawberries into fairly thick pieces.
4 Peel and slice the banana.
5 Mix the ingredients together and divide between four glasses. Garnish with the lemon twists and serve.

TIP BOX

An unripe banana contains more starch than sugar and, as it ripens, it has increasingly more sugar than starch. The colour of the skin gives a good indication as to its ripeness: green/yellow bananas tend to be high in starch while yellow/brown bananas are high in sugars.

Jolly Jesters

These stunning little numbers remind me of 'jolly jesters' because of their general colours and appearance. They look just like the harlequin patterns that jesters wear at court. Everyone is impressed with this unusual looking dessert that is quick and easy to make and low in calories. It's a winner.

Ingredients: Imperial/Metric

1 pkt	sugar-free wild strawberry jelly
4oz/100g	mixed red fruits
4fl oz/125ml	low fat natural yoghurt
1 pkt	sugar-free orange jelly
1	orange (zest)

Richard Proof

Serves: 6
Calories: 31
Preparation Time: 25 minutes
Chilling Time: 1 hour

Garnish:

6   redcurrant sprigs
6   fresh mint sprigs

Method:

1   Make the strawberry jelly by dissolving in 200ml of boiling water. Leave to cool.
2   Wash and prepare the fruit – keeping the fruit in bite-sized pieces.
3   Divide the fruit between 6 tall glasses and pour on the strawberry jelly. Leave the glasses tilted in a refrigerator to set for about 30 minutes.
4   Make the orange jelly by dissolving in 100ml of boiling water. Leave to cool.
5   Mix the yoghurt and zest of orange together and then pour into the jelly. Mix well.
6   Once the yoghurt mixture is quite cool, spoon onto the 'set' jellied fruits and place into the refrigerator for 30 minutes to set in an upright position.
7   Garnish with the redcurrant and mint sprigs.

Swap Shop Recipe
Days of Wine and Roses

The colourful layers of fruit and bread make this dish an attractive choice for guests. They'd never guess how simple it is to make!

Richard Proof
Cooking Time: 10 minutes

Serves: 8   *Preparation Time*: 35 minutes
Chilling Time: Overnight

Traditional version

Calories: 321

Ingredients: Imperial/Metric

1 lb 2oz/500g	mixed summer fruits, washed and prepared
6oz/175g	caster sugar
8	slices white bread, crusts removed
11 fl oz/300ml	double cream

Healthier version

Calories: 100

Ingredients: Imperial/Metric

1 lb 2oz/500g	mixed summer fruits, washed and prepared
2oz/50g	honey
8	slices wholemeal bread, crusts removed
11 fl oz/300ml	*fromage frais*

Method:

Place the fruit in a pan with the honey and gently bring to a boil. Simmer until the juices just begin to run and the fruit begins to break up.

Cut 3 circles of bread to fit the base, middle and top of a 2pt/900ml pudding basin.

Shape the remaining bread to fit around the sides of the basin.

Line the base and sides of the basin with the bread, spooning a little fruit in to keep the bread in place.

Spoon in enough fruit to come halfway up the sides of the basin.

Pour in some of the juice and cover with a circle of bread. Spoon in the remaining fruit and add some juice.

Cover with the remaining circle of bread and a saucer small enough to just fit inside the basin. Place a weight on the top – about 1 lb 2oz/500g should be sufficient.

Leave in the refrigerator overnight.

Turn out onto a serving plate and pour any remaining juice over the top. Serve with the *fromage frais*.

Food of the Pharaohs

Close scrutiny of ancient wall paintings in many Egyptian temples will reveal dried fruit. In fact, the use of dried fruit dates back to the time of the Pharaohs. Dried fruit contains many useful mineral and vitamins – the B vitamins are well represented and this is especially good for your appearance as they improve the condition of the hair, making it thick and shiny. I must admit that I would rather eat B vitamins to keep my hair looking and feeling good than douse it with paraffin. Believe it or not I read that tip in an old beauty book and a warning was printed by the side which read 'Avoid all naked lights . . . ' The mind boggles, doesn't it?

Not only nutritious and fibre-filled, this dessert is particularly low in calories. The cinnamon and lemon give it that extra zest!

Ingredients: Imperial/Metric

4oz/100g	dried prunes
4oz/100g	dried figs
4oz/100g	dried hunza apricots
4oz/100g	dried apples
2	lemons (zest and juice)
1½pt/575ml	soaking liquid (and water if necessary)
1in./2.5cm	cinnamon stick
1tsp	ground ginger

Richard Proof

Serves:	8
Calories:	37
Soaking Time:	Overnight
Preparation Time:	20 minutes
Cooking Time:	15 minutes

Garnish:
8   lemon twists

Method:
1. Soak the fruit overnight with plenty of cold water.
2. Drain the dried fruits and reserve the liquid.
3. Place the liquid, cinnamon and ginger in a pan and bring to a boil. Add the lemon juice and zest.
4. Add the dried fruits to the pan, cover and simmer for about 15 minutes.
5. Remove the cinnamon stick.
6. Spoon into individual serving dishes and garnish with the lemon twists. This dessert is wonderful eaten either hot or cold.

TIP BOX
Dried fruits should be cooked in the water in which they were soaked. This way you retain the nutrients and flavour.

Bishop's Mitres

What impressive little desserts these are. By using only pale yellow and white fruits a very subtle elegance is given to these mouth-watering 'moulds'. I set the fruits in wine glasses and then upturn them onto a serving plate. They remind Richard of a Bishop's hat – or mitre, if we use the correct term – hence the name of this recipe.

Ingredients: Imperial/Mitre

7fl oz/200ml	medium-dry white wine
11fl oz/300ml	clear white grape juice
3fl oz/75ml	clear apple juice
1	passion fruit, seeds and flesh
6	lychees, halved and stoned
1oz/25g	kumquats, washed and sliced
2	peaches, skinned and sliced
1	star fruit, washed and thinly sliced
1oz/25g	gelatin

Richard Proof

Serving:	6
Calories:	77
Preparation Time:	25 minutes
Chilling Time:	2 hours

Garnish:

6	lavender heads
12	lime wings

Method:

1   Boil 4fl oz/125ml water and stir in the gelatin until completely dissolved. Stir in the grape juice, wine and apple juice. Leave to cool.
2   With your six wine glasses in front of you, start arranging the fruit around the edge of the glasses – star fruit look beautiful pressed against the glass and a lychee looks nice jammed right down at the base.
3   As you pile in the fruit, gradually start to pour the wine mixture in – just enough to cover the fruit you have placed.
4   Leave to set for about 2 hours.
5   Rinse the glasses under hot running water to loosen the set at the edge of the glasses and turn out onto serving plates.
6   Garnish with lavender heads and lime wings.

> **TIP BOX**
> Every part of the kumquat can be eaten – the skin, pips and flesh.

Hippocrates

Every single part of the papaya, including its seeds, leaves and tree bark, have legendary medicinal properties. In fact, many parts of Africa and the Carribean use it as a staple part of their medicine chest, rather than food cupboard. Would you believe it cures anything from ear aches to burns? Quite an impressive fruit is papaya. Combined with kumquats and lychees, papaya gives this dessert an international flavour. This dish is not only easy and quick to prepare, but it has only 25 calories per serving!

Ingredients: Imperial/Metric
1	papaya, peeled
4	lychees, peeled
4oz/100g	kumquats, washed

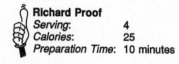

Richard Proof
Serving: 4
Calories: 25
Preparation Time: 10 minutes

Garnish:
4   sprigs of mint

Method:
1 Cut the kumquats in half.
2 Chop the papaya into even-sized pieces.
3 Cut the lychees in half and discard the stones.
4 Mix all of the fruit together very well and pile into glass serving dishes. Garnish with mint sprigs.

> **TIP BOX**
> The next time you suffer from a digestive problem try eating the seeds of a papaya. In many countries these are ground and made into stomach pills.

My Darling Clementine

Unfortunately I just happened to mention to Richard that I was going to name a dessert 'My Darling Clementine'. For days, literally, he just kept on singing and whistling that tune made famous by the old western. Both the guests staying at Harrow Ings and I were fed up listening to it! It nearly drove one poor woman who was suffering from tinnitus, bonkers. The orange water adds a fragrant touch to this fruity salad. It's the perfect end to a heavy meal.

Ingredients: Imperial/Metric
2	clementines, peeled
4	apricots, skinned
2	passion fruit
2	fresh figs, washed
1tbsp	orange flower water

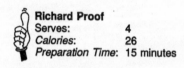

Richard Proof
Serves: 4
Calories: 26
Preparation Time: 15 minutes

Garnish:

4   fresh sprigs of mint

Method:

1   Segment the clementines.
2   Slice the apricots and remove the stones.
3   Cut the passion fruit in half and scoop out the flesh and seeds.
4   Quarter the figs (I never peel figs as I think it ruins the taste and texture).
5   Mix all the fruits together and arrange on four nice serving plates.
6   Spoon over the orange flower water and garnish with the mint.

> **TIP BOX**
> The addition of rosewater or orange flower water not only imparts a refreshing, delicate taste to the fruit but also adds a lovely aroma.

Marco Polo

When Marco Polo's sailors became ill with scurvy they were given papaya to eat and it saved their lives. Papaya does have a high vitamin C content. This selection of fruit looks wonderful simply served on a plain white plate to show off the subtle differences in shades. The tang of the grapefruit gives a nice contrast to the mellow tasting papaya – a beautiful combination.

Ingredients: Imperial/Metric
1   papaya, peeled
1   ruby grapefruit
2   peaches, skinned

Richard Proof
Serves: 4
Calories: 28
Preparation Time: 10 minutes

Garnish:
4   nasturtium flowers

Method:
1   Peel the grapefruit and segment it – removing the membrane from the pieces.
2   Slice the peaches in narrow wedge shapes.
3   Cut the papaya in half lengthways and remove the seeds. Turn the papaya flat side down and slice into narrow pieces lengthways.
4   Arrange slices of papaya on four serving plates. Place a layer of grapefruit segments just overlapping the papaya and finish with a slightly overlapping layer of peach slices.
5   Garnish each with a nasturtium flower.

Archangel's Wings

Angelica is a herb with possesses a lovely sweet flavour and is generally very useful in cooking. You will have seen the crystallized stalks of angelica which are used for decoration and to flavour cakes and creams. Chopped and sprinkled over fruit salads, fresh angelica really adds a new dimension to the dish.
Angelica was supposedly blessed by St Michael the Archangel – hence the name of this recipe. This fruit extravagaza looks absolutely spectacular.

Richard Proof
Serving: 4
Calories: 67
Preparation Time: 20 minutes

Ingredients: Imperial/Metric
2   small galia melons
1   kiwi, washed
4oz/100g   green grapes, seedless, washed
3   lychees, peeled
1   red apple, washed
1tbsp   fresh angelica , washed and chopped

Garnish:

4   fresh angelica leaves
8   orange wings

Method:

1   The idea is to make a scalloped pattern around the melon at both ends and to use these 'shells' as serving dishes. If, like me, you find it difficult to do this freehand then do what I do – use a coin. All you have to do is hold the coin against the melon, about one-third of the way up, and draw pencil lines on the top edge of the coin – making sure that the edges meet. This gives you a continuous scalloped tracing line to follow. With a sharp knife, cut through the melon to the centre, following the tracing line. Discard the seeds and 'melon ball' the centre pieces of melon that are left.

2   Slice the kiwi fruit.

3   Slice the apple.

4   Cut the lychee into slices.

5   Mix the fruit together and add the chopped angelica. Pile into the melon 'shells' and garnish with the angelica leaves and orange twists.

TIP BOX
Passion fruit is full of black seeds which you eat along with the pulp. The fibre content of passion fruit is therefore high.

Bedouin

Dates are one of the oldest cultivated fruits, popular for over seven thousand years. The date palm will often grow where nothing else will – even in deserts. Because of its versatility, the date is an important part of the Bedouin diet and provides a drinking liqueur, as well as a sweetening agent. The flavour of the dates and figs soaks into the apples, sweetening them naturally – and there are only 54 calories per stuffed apple!

Ingredients: Imperial/Metric

4	cooking apples
2oz/50g	dates, chopped
1oz/25g	figs, chopped
4tbsp	apple juice

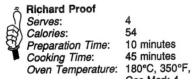

Richard Proof

Serves:	4
Calories:	54
Preparation Time:	10 minutes
Cooking Time:	45 minutes
Oven Temperature:	180°C, 350°F, Gas Mark 4

Method:

1   Core the apples.

2   Make a shallow cut around the centre of each one – this stops the apples from splitting open during cooking.

3   Mix together the dates and figs.

4   Fill the apple cavities with the mixture and press down firmly.

5   Place in an oven-proof dish and pour over the apple juice. Bake until apples are just soft.

Swap Shop Recipe
Isle of Honey

Honey, with its long and varied past, has been associated with many people and countries. At the time of the Druids, Ancient Britain was known as the Isle of Honey. The reason for this label was the vast quantities of honey Britons consumed – especially in the form of mead! This fruity dessert doesn't contain honey, but its natural sweetness suggests the succulent treat. Since it serves 8, this moulded mousse is ideal for company.

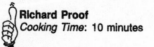 **Richard Proof**   *Serves:* 8   *Preparation Time:* 30 minutes
Cooking Time: 10 minutes   *Chilling Time:* 1 hour

Traditional version		*Healthier version*	
Calories: 290		Calories: 71	
Ingredients: Imperial/Metric		**Ingredients:** Imperial/Metric	
35fl oz/850ml	water	35fl oz/850ml	water
8oz/225g	sugar		not required
3	lemons (zest and juice)	3	lemons (zest and juice)
2tsp	ground cinnamon	1 in./2.5cm	cinnamon stick
1¹/₂oz/40g	gelatin	1¹/₂oz/40g	gelatin
4tbsp	sweet sherry		not required
6oz/175g	black grapes, seeded	6oz/175g	black grapes, seeded
6oz/175g	green grapes, seeded	6oz/175g	green grapes, seeded
7fl oz/200ml	double cream, whipped	7fl oz/200ml	*fromage frais*
		1tsp	vanilla essence

Method:

Put the grape juice, lemon zest and juice, and cinnamon stick in a pan and heat gently.

Dissolve the gelatin in 3 tablespoons of boiling water and add to the grape juice. Stir well.

Remove the cinnamon stick and pour a little of the juice into a 2pt/1.2 litre ring mould and chill in the refrigerator until set.

Arrange some black grapes on the surface and cover with juice. Leave to set. Add another layer of juice, leave to set, and arrange green grapes on the surface.

Continue this process until the mould is full. Place back in the refrigerator

until set. Mix together the *fromage frais* and vanilla essence and put aside to garnish.
Turn out onto a serving plate and decorate with the *fromage frais* and vanilla mixture.

Red-hot Pokers

This dessert looks stunning and tastes out of this world. Succulent, translucent pears, glazed with a red sauce, standing to attention on a serving plate. What a feast for eyes and taste buds.

Ingredients: Imperial/Metric

6	dessert pears
5fl oz/150ml	red grape juice
5fl oz/150ml	red wine
1 in./2.5cm	cinnamon stick
2tsp	arrowroot

Richard Proof

Serves:	6
Calories:	75
Preparation Time:	20 minutes
Cooking Time:	30 minutes

Garnish:

6	sprigs of fresh mint
2tbsp	low fat natural yoghurt

Method:

1   Place the wine, grape juice and cinnamon in a pan. Bring to the boil and boil for 5 minutes.
2   Peel the pears but leave their stalks intact. Place the pears in the pan with the wine mixture and simmer gently for 20 minutes. Discard the cinnamon stick.
3   Arrange the pears on a serving dish – as if the pears were standing to attention.
4   Mix the arrowroot with a little water and add to the wine. Stir continuously until the mixture thickens and becomes clear. This should only take a minute or two of gentle boiling.
5   Spoon the wine mixture over and around the pears. Drop little spirals of yoghurt into the red mixture and garnish with mint. These pears can be served either hot or cold.

TIP BOX
Always use fruit of the highest quality in fruit salads.

Sweetheart

Traditionally, pavlovas are heavily laden with sugar but it doesn't always have to be the case. In this pavlova, the base is low in sugar making it a little stickier than the traditional dish, but that's how I like it. It is a wonderful display of vivid colours and shapes – a real treat.

Ingredients: Imperial/Metric

4	egg whites
6oz/75g	brown sugar
1tsp	vinegar
2tbsp	cornflour
14oz/400g	fresh fruits, washed and prepared
11fl oz/300ml	Greek strained yoghurt

Richard Proof

Serves:	8
Calories:	120
Preparation Time:	30 minutes
Cooking Time:	90 minutes
Oven Temperature:	150°C, 300°F, Gas Mark 2

Method:

1 Beat the egg whites with the vinegar until stiff.
2 Gradually add the sugar, whisking constantly.
3 Very carefully fold in the cornflour.
4 Spoon the mixture onto a lined, lightly oiled baking sheet. (I like to make a heart shape with the mixture about 7 in./18cm long). Then hollow out the centre – giving you room to place the fruit when the base is cooked.
5 Bake the base for about $1^1/_2$ hours and cool under a cloth. Remove the lining paper very carefully to avoid breaking the base.
6 Spoon the yoghurt into the centre of the heart and then fill with the fruit.

Apple John

A very attractive-looking layered dessert which is best shown off when served in a glass.

Ingredients: Imperial/Metric

8oz/225g	blackberries, washed
1 lb 2oz/500g	dessert apples, washed and cored
4oz/100g	oat-bran flakes
4oz/100g	wholemeal bread-crumbs, toasted
2tbsp	crème de cassis

Richard Proof

Serves:	4
Calories:	223
Preparation Time:	15 minutes
Cooking Time:	5 minutes
Can be frozen	

Method:

1 Place the blackberries and chopped apple in a pan with the crème de cassis and heat gently for about 5 minutes – just until the apple begins to soften and the juices run. Let cool.

2 Divide half the fruit between four individual glasses and cover with half the oat flakes and breadcrumbs. Repeat the layers.

3 Serve chilled.

Hedgehog

I first saw mango prepared like a 'hedgehog' when we were in Thailand; it looked so impressive that I asked the Thai cook to show me how to do it. Thailand is well know for fruit sculpture – it takes many, many years of training to tackle the more elaborate designs.

Ingredients:

2 mangoes
12 strawberries
4 kiwi fruit

Richard Proof
Serves: 4
Calories: 45
Preparation Time: 30 minutes

Garnish:

4 attractive flowers
4 sprigs of fresh mint

Method:

1 Carefully take a slice from each side of the large flat stone of the mango. Without cutting right through the skin, make diagonal cuts along the inside of the slice and repeat the cuts in the opposite direction. Do exactly the same thing with the remaining three slices. Hold the mango slice in your hands and gently push the skin side upwards – making a hollow underneath. You are now left with a hedgehog look-alike.

2 Cut the kiwi fruit 'Van Dyke' style.

3 Serve on individual plates and garnish attractively with the strawberries cut into fans (see below).

TIP BOX

To make strawberry fans, simply cut four slices from just beneath the hull of the strawberry to the bottom. Gently spread the fan slices out. This is an attractive and colourful garnish for ice cream, mousses or fresh fruit salads.

Exotica

I love exotic fruit salads when they are presented with a little flair and imagination. You can use any kind of fruit in this dessert but I like fresh figs and passion fruit to be included as they give a different texture to the combination of fruit.

Ingredients:
4   fresh figs, washed
6   kumquats, washed
1   papaya
1   star fruit, washed
2   passion fruits
8   lychees
1   red apple

Richard Proof
Serves: 4
Calories: 50
Preparation Time: 30 minutes

Garnish:
8   sprigs of mint
8   sprigs of blue lobelia

Method:
1   Cut the figs into quarters – but do not cut through the base, leave a 'hinge' of about $^3/_4$ in./6mm.
2   Thinly slice the star fruit.
3   Cut the passion fruit and kumquats 'Van Dyke' style – using a sharp knife make zig zag cuts around the centre of each fruit going right through to the centre. You are left with attractive points around the fruits. Tomatoes are often associated with this kind of presentation.
4   Cut the papaya in half lengthways and scoop out the seeds. Slice the papaya about 1 in./2.5cm thick widthways.
5   Carefully cut through the skin of the lychees going right around their circumference. Pull the bottom half away from the fruit leaving the top intact. The lychees should now resemble acorns.
6   Cut the apple into wedges or 'wings', using the method described in the Tip Box on page 28.
7   Arrange the shapes attractively on individual plates – use large plates so that the fruit isn't cramped. Garnish with blue lobelia and mint.

Fluted Fancies

These little carob 'cups' look absolutely delightful and give that elegant touch to the dessert. The filling is very low in fat and uses only the natural sweetness of the strawberries instead of sugar. The contrasting textures give an added dimension to the dish.

Ingredients: Imperial/Metric

4	paper bun cases
2oz/50g	sugar-free carob bar
2oz/50g	strawberries, hulled and halved
4fl oz/100ml	*fromage frais*
1tsp/5g	gelatin

Not Richard Proof
Richard made a real mess of this one. He just couldn't make the carob 'cups'. I think the problem was that he tried to take the bun case off in a hurry destroying the cups in the process.

Serves: 4
Calories: 54
Preparation Time: 45 minutes
Chilling Time: 45 minutes

Garnish:
4   colourful flowers
4   strawberries

Method:
1. Break the carob into pieces and place in a small bowl over a pan of hot water. Stir until melted.
2. Carefully brush the inside of each bun case with the melted carob – don't leave any gaps or thin parts. The top is the most easily broken so brush the carob on a little thicker towards the top edge.
3. Leave to cool and set in the refrigerator for about 30 minutes.
4. Liquidize half of the strawberries with 1 tablespoon of the *fromage frais.*
5. Carefully fold in the remaining *fromage frais* and strawberries.
6. Dissolve the gelatin in 1 tablespoon of boiling water and stir into the strawberry mixture. Leave to set in the refrigerator for 45 minutes.
7. Carefully remove the paper bun case from the carob. The easiest way to do this is to loosen the fluted parts at the lop and then carefully and slowly peel the bun case off.
8. Place a generous portion of the strawberry mixture into each carob cup and garnish.

TIP BOX
Never allow water to splash from the pan into the carob as it will cause the mixture to become dry and grainy.

Chapter Six
Fromage to Cheesecake

I was just coming towards the end of a healthy cookery demonstration at Luton Hoo when someone from the audience exclaimed, 'Come off it. That isn't healthy'. The dish in question was a very elaborate strawberry cheesecake. I can understand the apparent contradiction in terms for it looked every bit as rich, creamy and naughty as a normal everyday cheesecake. Without replying to the doubting Thomas I offered pieces of the cheesecake to the audience for them to taste. The verdict was unanimous. The strawberry cheesecake could definitely not be healthy. With a pained expression on my face I asked, 'Why can't it be healthy?' 'It tastes too good,' was the reply. Needless to say the cheesecake didn't last very long. Everyone loved it. One very nice elderly lady, who confessed to being somewhat of an expert, paid me the compliment of saying that my cheesecake was the best she had ever tasted.

Then came the task of convincing my sceptical audience – who by this time were really digging in to the food – that my cheesecake was healthy. I demonstrated my technique and began to swap the unhealthy cheesecake ingredients with healthy alternatives and there we had it – a healthy cheesecake. My audience were very impressed and, more importantly, convinced. Apparently I am now famous for my cheesecakes amongst the organizers of the event!

Many people will be surprised, and some horrified, to find such things as cheesecakes in a book concerned with healthy eating. Cheesecakes are beautifully rich and creamy and these are the very qualities that make them so popular with people. The full fat cream cheese, double cream, egg yolks and sugar all create the rich taste. However, these ingredients also make the cheesecake very high in fat – especially the saturated variety – very high in cholesterol and simply loaded with calories. Traditional cheesecakes are, therefore, a health hazard.

My cheesecakes are every bit as rich and creamy as any you will find in a classy restaurant and they certainly look just as impressive. The difference is that my cheesecakes are low in fat and cholesterol and contain far fewer calories than the traditional cakes. Cheesecakes definitely don't have to be banned because of their adverse effect on our health.

The process is simple. All you have to do is swap some of the unhealthy ingredients for healthier ones and suddenly you have developed a cheesecake which is not only healthy but even lighter and more delicious. To give you an idea of how this works I have included a couple of 'Swap Shop' recipes to help you. I use low fat soft cheese or tofu instead of full fat soft cheeses. The cream is replaced with either silken tofu, fromage frais or low fat yoghurt. These simple yet effective changes really cut down the fat and calorie content of the cheesecake without altering the flavour and texture. The sugar content of a cheesecake is quite high both in the base and topping but you can use fruit zest, various fruits (such as bananas) and honey to sweeten instead. This way you not only reduce the calories but also add important nutrients. The fibre content is increased by using cereals and seeds in the base and fresh fruit in the filling.

The cheesecake is often thought of as being a modern dessert and yet it has a long history and tradition. Believe it or not, cheesecakes were as popular in the thirteenth century as they are today. Cottage cheese was used in the early days with egg yolks and sugar. A couple of centuries later, lemons and dried fruits were added. The digestive base and cream cheese filling has its roots in America and some friends of ours, from Boston on the East coast, boast that New Yorkers make the best cheesecakes in the world!

Huckleberry Finn

In America the bilberry is often called a huckleberry, whortleberry or blueberry – confusing isn't it? This cheesecake is my favourite. Bilberries are a beautiful soft fruit which I have loved for as long as I can remember. My Mum and Dad used to take me 'bilberrying' when I was a little girl – it was a smashing day out. You used to see whole families with their forks and basins collecting these delectable little fruits.

Now we live in the country with bilberry bushes on our doorstep and in seven years we haven't managed to harvest any. The birds or other bilberry pickers always beat us to it!

The colours and marbled effect of this cheesecake looks absolutely stunning.

Ingredients: Imperial/Metric

2	spun wheat biscuits, crushed
1tbsp	honey
5oz/150ml	firm silken tofu, liquidized
11fl oz/300ml	*fromage frais*
8oz/225g	fresh wild bilberries
1tbsp	apple juice
4tsp	Gelozone

Garnish:

4oz/100g	fresh wild bilberries
2tsp	Gelozone
1tbsp	apple juice
3	orange wings
1	fresh mint sprig

Not Richard Proof
Difficulty with the marbled effect – he mixed the fruit in too well. It tasted lovely though.

Serves:	8
Calories:	85
Preparation Time:	35 minutes
Cooking Time:	10 minutes
Chilling Time:	5 hours
Oven Temperature:	200°C, 400°F, Gas Mark 5

Can be frozen

60

Method:

1 Mix the honey and spun wheat biscuits together and press firmly into the base of an 8 in./20cm, loose-bottomed cake tin. Bake for 10 minutes.

2 Mix together the tofu and *fromage frais*.

3 Gently heat the bilberries and apple juice until the bilberries just begin to lose their juices. Leave to cool.

4 Sprinkle the Gelozone onto the bilberry mixture and whisk in well. Heat gently until steam begins to rise from the pan. Do not allow to boil. Leave to cool for about 10 minutes.

5 Gradually pour half the bilberry mixture into the cheese and tofu – mix well. Pour in the remaining half being very careful not to mix it in well. You should have pink and deep purple patches.

6 Pile this mixture into the cake tin and chill for 3 hours.

7 Make the topping as in 3 and 4 above, but leave to cool for 20 minutes. Spoon this mixture on top of the cheesecake and chill for 2 hours until set. Garnish with mint and wings.

TIP BOX

Never pour a hot glaze over a set cheesecake as it will make deep cracks in it. This happened to me with a cheesecake which was to appear on television. It looked like Mount Etna. However, the film crew and subsequent viewers were most impressed and asked how to achieve such a stunning effect with the glaze! And, yes, I did own up.

Karyon

Greeks call walnuts 'karyon', kara meaning head, because it looks like a human brain. And it does, doesn't it?

I wanted a base that was nutty and cake-like and yet low in calories and fat. The result was this one. The sweetness is drawn from the dates and the carob, and the fat content is cut by using walnuts. Try using redcurrants, raspberries or blackberries to alter this very versatile cheesecake.

Ingredients: Imperial/Metric

2oz/50g	dried dates
3fl oz/70ml	water
1oz/25g	carob powder
1oz/25g	plain wholemeal flour
1tsp	low-sodium baking powder
1oz/25g	walnuts, broken
5oz/150g	quark
5fl oz/150ml	firm silken tofu, liquidized
5fl oz/150ml	low fat natural set yoghurt

Richard Proof

Serves:	10
Calories:	80
Preparation Time:	45 minutes
Cooking Time:	15 minutes
Chilling Time:	2 hours
Oven Temperature:	180°C, 350°F, Gas Mark 4

Can be frozen

Garnish:

8oz/225g	blackcurrants
2tsp	Gelozone
1tbsp	honey
8	walnuts
2oz/50g	low fat set yoghurt
8	lemon twists

Method:

1 Put the dates and water into a saucepan and simmer until the dates are soft and pulpy. Leave to cool.

2 Sift the flour, baking powder and carob into a bowl and add the walnuts and date mixture.

3 Spoon into a greased 7 in./18cm tin and bake for about 15 minutes until it feels spongy to the touch. Leave to cool.

4 Liquidize the tofu with 1 tablespoon of the yoghurt.

5 Mix together the yoghurt, tofu mixture and quark.

6 Spoon the mixture onto the base and place in the refrigerator for at least 60 minutes until set.

7 Place the blackcurrants and honey in a small pan and add the Gelozone – mixing it in very well. Heat through until the mixture begins to steam. Do not allow to boil.

8　Allow the blackcurrants to cool and then spoon over the cheesecake.

9　Keep in the refrigerator for at least 60 minutes to set.

10　Garnish with the yoghurt, lemon twists and walnuts.

Swap Shop Recipe
Hades and Minthe

Greek legend tells of a Greek nymph called Minthe who was loved by Hades. Persephone, Hades' wife, was jealous and ground the nymph into the earth. Heartbroken Hades found the spot of earth where Minthe lay and turned her remains into the plant Mint, which could grow on forever. It is alleged that for this reason mint grows in abundance and is universally loved. Hence the name of this recipe.

I invented this recipe for a dear friend of ours who loves chocolate and cheesecakes but hates the calories and fat content. She and her husband were coming up from London for the weekend and I decided to make this after dinner treat. It certainly got the 'Sally' seal of approval and proved to her that you can still eat chocolate-tasting cheesecakes without the fat and calories! This stunning layered cheesecake has swirls of carob chocolate to add that finishing touch.

 Richard Proof　　*Serves*: 8　　*Chilling Time*: 3 hours
Preparation Time: 30 minutes　　　*Cooking Time*: 15 minutes
Oven Temperature: 200°C, 400°F, Gas Mark 6　　*Can be frozen*

Traditional version

Calories: 628

Healthier version

Calories: 164

Ingredients: Imperial/Metric

2oz/50g	butter
4oz/125g	chocolate digestive biscuits, crushed
4oz/125g	plain chocolate, melted

Ingredients: Imperial/Metric

1tbsp	honey
3	Wholewheat cereal biscuits, crushed
1oz/25g	sugar-free carob bar, plain
4oz/125g	sugar-free mint flavoured carob bar, melted

4tbsp	milk	4tsp	skimmed milk
3oz/175g	full fat soft cheese	6fl oz/175ml	firm silken tofu, liquidized
8oz/225ml	double cream, whipped	8fl oz/225ml	*fromage frais*
3oz/75g	sugar	1tbsp	honey
1/2tsp	peppermint essence		not required
1/2oz/15g	gelatin	1/2oz/15g	gelatin

Topping:

7fl oz/250ml	double cream, whipped	7fl oz/250ml	low fat natural yoghurt
1oz/25g	chocolate curls	1oz/25g	sugar-free carob bar
		1/2oz/11g	gelatin

Method:

Melt the honey and stir in the wholewheat biscuit crumbs. Line the base of the 8 in./20cm loose-bottomed cake tin and cook for 10 minutes. Leave to cool.

Melt the plain carob in a small bowl over a pan of hot water and stir until dissolved. Pour over the biscuit mixture.

Melt the mint carob with the milk in a bowl over a pan of hot water.

Place the cheese and tofu in a bowl and blend in the carob.

Place the gelatin in 3 tablespoons of boiling water to dissolve. Cool slightly and then stir into the carob mixture.

Fold the *fromage frais* into the mixture and spoon over the biscuit base. Chill in the refrigerator until set.

Dissolve the remaining gelatine in 2 tablespoons of boiling water and allow to cool slightly before adding to the yoghurt.

Pour this mixture onto the cheesecake.

Melt the carob over a pan of hot water. When melted, drop spoonfuls onto the cheesecake top and then quickly make swirling patterns in the carob and yoghurt using a fork.

Leave to set for 1 hour. Carefully remove the cheeesecake from the tin.

TIP BOX

To make carob quills simply break 3oz/175g of carob bar into a bowl and place over a pan of hot water. Once it has melted pour it on to a flat surface – marble is excellent as it is both smooth and cold. Spread the carob thinly and evenly. As soon as the carob sets run a sharp knife across it making quills.

Bali Sunrise

A wonderfully rich and creamy cheesecake that tastes as though it's really bad for your health. I made this particular cheesecake for one of my appearances on 'The Miriam Stoppard Show'. Some unsuspecting shoppers in a leading supermarket were asked to taste it – the response was marvellous. Everyone wanted to know how to make this cheesecake – including the film crew! The Indonesian island of Bali is known as 'the morning of the world' and has spectacular sunrises with bright and vibrant colours. A perfect name for this cheesecake!

Ingredients: Imperial/Metric

11oz/300g	low fat soft cheese
5fl oz/150ml	firm tofu
1/2tsp	vanilla essence
1	sugar-free jelly, orange flavour
4fl oz/125ml	boiling water
1	orange (zest)
2oz/50g	rolled oats
2oz/50g	sugar-free bran flakes
2oz/50g	sunflower seeds
2tbsp	honey

Garnish:

1	orange
4	strawberries
1	sugar-free jelly, orange flavour
4fl oz/125ml	boiling water

Richard Proof

Serves:	8
Calories:	120
Preparation Time:	25 minutes
Cooking Time:	20 minutes
Chilling Time:	2 hours
Oven Temperature:	200°C, 400°F, Gas Mark 6

Can be frozen

> **TIP BOX**
> Oats are wonderful as they are high in soluble fibre and polyunsaturated oils. Oats have been found to be extremely useful in reducing blood cholesterol levels, particularly the LDL type.

Method:

1. Mix together the seeds, bran flakes, oats and honey. Place into an 8in./20cm loose-bottomed cake tin and press down firmly.
2. Bake in a pre-heated oven for about 20 minutes. Leave to cool.
3. Mix one packet of jelly with 4fl oz/150ml of boiling water and stir until the jelly has dissolved completely Leave to cool in the refrigerator.
4. Liquidize the tofu until it's fairly smooth.
5. Mix together the cheese and tofu. Add the orange zest.
6. Gradually stir the jelly into the cheese mixture.
7. Pour the cheese mixture onto the seed base and leave to set in the refrigerator for about an hour.
8. Dissolve the remaining packet of jelly in 4fl oz/150ml of boiling water and leave it to cool for 30 minutes.
9. Once the cheesecake has set, pour the orange jelly on the top and leave to set for about an hour in the refrigerator.
10. Garnish with orange wings and strawberry fans.

Cassia

Cassia is a spice from the same family as cinnamon and is often sold in its place. Cassia is far cheaper than cinnamon but the flavour isn't as good. Cassia is lighter in colour than cinnamon. I love the flavours of cinnamon and orange mingling together in this baked cheesecake. The texture is rich and creamy – it melts in your mouth.

Ingredients: Imperial/Metric

5oz/150g	wholemeal flour
3oz/75g	polyunsaturated, unhydrogenated margarine
1oz/25g	raw cane sugar
8oz/225g	low fat soft cheese
8fl oz/225ml	firm silken tofu
1tbsp	honey
5fl oz/150ml	*fromage frais*
2tsp	ground cinnamon
3	egg whites

Richard Proof

Serves:	8
Calories:	214
Preparation Time:	35 minutes
Cooking Time:	60 minutes
Oven Temperature:	160°C, 325°F, Gas Mark 3

Can be frozen

Garnish:

3fl oz/75ml	*fromage frais*
2tsp	ground cinnamon

Method:

1 Sift the flour into a bowl and rub in the margarine.
2 Add the sugar and press the mixture into a firm dough. Knead until fairly smooth.
3 Liquidize the tofu with the honey.
4 Beat the soft cheese in a bowl and add the tofu mixture.
5 Carefully mix in the *fromage frais* and cinnamon.
6 Whisk the egg whites until stiff and carefully fold into the mixture.
7 Grease and line an 8 in./20cm loose-bottomed cake tin and press the crumb mixture firmly to the base and side.
8 Spoon in the cheese mixture and bake for about 60 minutes. Leave to cool in the tin.
9 Garnish with the *fromage frais* and cinnamon.

TIP BOX

If you find that your firm tofu is just too solid to liquidize, add a little skimmed milk to aid the process.

Mistral

This is to say the least, a most unusual cheesecake. In fact, it isn't really a 'cake' at all, as the cheese and fig filling is stuffed into a wholemeal French stick. The rich creamy filling has a thick wedge of fig running through the whole length of the stick. The effect is stunning and is sure to impress.

Ingredients: Imperial/Metric

1	wholemeal French stick
5oz/150g	dried figs
6fl oz/175ml	apple juice
1	orange (zest)
6oz/175g	low fat soft cheese

Richard Proof

Serves:	8
Calories:	76
Soaking Time:	Overnight
Preparation Time:	40 minutes
Chilling Time:	1 day
Can be Frozen	

Garnish:
4   fresh strawberries
4   fresh figs
8   fresh mint sprigs

Method:
1   Soak the dried figs in the apple juice overnight.
2   Place in a pan and bring to a boil. Simmer for 5 minutes.
3   Leave to cool.
4   Liquidize the fig mixture and leave to cool for 15 minutes.
5   Mix together the cheese and the orange zest.
6   Make a slit down one of the long sides of the French stick until you are almost through to the other side. Hollow out the bread until you are left with a 'shell'.
7   Place half of the soft cheese mixture in the French stick 'shell' and half of the fig mixture on top of that.
8   Place the rest of the soft cheese mixture in the remaining French stick 'shell' followed by a layer of fig filling.
9   Sandwich the two 'shells' together and tie firmly to keep in place.
10 Freeze for 1 day and remove one hour before serving. Slice and serve garnished with fresh figs, strawberries and mint.

Tropicana

The ginger adds a lovely fresh taste to the cheesecake and compliments the subtle flavour of the bananas and soft cheese. The addition of the bananas not only gives a nice flavour but natural sweetness as well. The rose looks wonderful in the centre of the cheesecake and you could wax it to make it look even more attractive – it will last longer too. Do make sure your roses are free of greenflies!

Ingredients: Imperial/Metric

2oz/50g	sugar- and salt-free bran flakes
2oz/50g	oats
1oz/25g	toasted sesame seeds
2tsp	ground ginger
8oz/225g	low fat soft cheese
2tbsp	*fromage frais*
2	egg whites
2	pieces of stem ginger, chopped
1	banana, mashed

Richard Proof

Serves:	6
Calories:	108
Preparation Time:	30 minutes
Cooking Time:	50 minutes
Chilling Time:	60 minutes
Oven Temperature:	160°C, 325°F, Gas Mark 3

Can be frozen

Garnish:

1	banana
1tsp	ground ginger
8	fresh mint sprigs or borage leaves
1	yellow rose head with leaves

Method:

1 Mix together the first five ingredients and press firmly into a 6 in./15cm loose-bottomed cake tin. Cook for 20 minutes.
2 Blend together the *fromage frais* and soft cheese. Mix in the mashed banana and ginger.
3 Whisk the egg whites until stiff and carefully fold into the mixture.
4 Pour into the flan case and bake for about 30 minutes until firm and golden.
5 Allow to cool and then chill in the refrigerator. Sprinkle the ground ginger on top of the cheesecake and garnish with the sliced banana, ground ginger and mint or borage leaves. Place the rose head in the centre.

The Great Wall of China

The kiwi fruit originated in China before it was adopted by New Zealand. Greengages are a wonderful fruit that are terribly underrated in this country. They are lovely pale green in colour and have a nice sweet taste that doesn't overpower the fruit. The different shades of green look very attractive but to add more colour you could use strawberries or raspberries with the greengages. The orange sponge base gives it an added dimension – you'll love it.

Ingredients: Imperial/Metric

3oz/75g	plain wholemeal flour
1oz/25g	sugar
2tsp	low-sodium baking powder
2tbsp	sesame seed oil
3fl oz/75ml	water
1	orange (zest)
9oz/250g	ricotta cheese
9oz/250g	low fat soft cheese

Richard Proof

Serves:	10
Calories:	115
Preparation Time:	45 minutes
Cooking Time:	25 minutes
Chilling Time:	Overnight
Oven Temperature:	190°C, 375°F, Gas Mark 5

Can be frozen

Garnish:

6oz/175g	greengages, washed, halved and stoned
1	kiwi fruit, washed and sliced

Method:

1. Mix the first six ingredients together and press into the base of an 8in./20cm loose-bottomed cake tin. Bake for 20 minutes.
2. Mix the ricotta cheese and low fat soft cheese together.
3. Spoon onto the base and leave to set in the refrigerator overnight.
4. Arrange the slices of kiwi around the edge of the cheesecake and place the greengages in the centre.

TIP BOX

Fruits are often sprayed not only with herbicides and pesticides but with wax as well. That's why most oranges and apples look very shiny. So always wash fruit very well in either soapy water or cider vinegar.

Swap Shop Recipe
Solomon's Nectar

Honey has a long and interesting history and it is even mentioned in the Song of Solomon. The Israelites were promised a land 'flowing with milk and honey'. Nectar is collected from flowers by honey bees which is deposited in honeycombs where it is converted into honey. This cheesecake is deliciously rich – you'd never guess that it has only 20 per cent of the calories of the traditional version!

Not Richard Proof
Too heavy-handed when folding in the egg whites. He stirred out most of the air he had whisked into them in the first place! The cheesecake was a little heavier than it should be.

Serves:	8
Preparation Time:	40 minutes
Cooking Time:	15 minutes
Chilling Time:	2 hours
Oven Temperature:	200°C, 400°F, Gas Mark 6

Can be frozen

Traditional version

Calories: 490

Ingredients: Imperial/Metric

2oz/50g	butter
4oz/125g	digestive biscuits
4oz/125g	full fat soft cheese
4oz/125g	medium fat curd cheese
3oz/75g	caster sugar
1	lemon (rind and juice)
$1/_2$oz/15g	gelatin
2tbsp	water
11fl oz/300ml	double cream
3	egg whites
6oz/175g	raspberry pie filling
3fl oz/75ml	double cream

Healthier version

Calories: 99

Ingredients: Imperial/Metric

1tbsp	honey
3	wholewheat cereal biscuits, crushed
8oz/225g	low fat soft cheese
4oz/125g	*fromage frais*
1oz/25g	honey
1	lemon (rind and juice)
$1/_2$oz/15g	gelatin
2tbsp	water
4fl oz/125ml	firm silken tofu
3	egg whites
4fl oz/100g	fresh raspberries
3fl oz/75ml	*fromage frais*

Method:
Melt the honey and add it to the crushed wholewheat cereal biscuits. Press into the base of an 8 in./20cm, loose-bottomed cake tin. Cook for 10 minutes and leave to cool.

Place the cheeses in a bowl and blend in the lemon, rind and juice.

Soak the gelatin in the water in a bowl. Place the bowl over a pan of gently simmering water and stir until dissolved. Cool slightly, then stir into the cheese mixture.

Whip the firm tofu until it resembles whipped cream and fold into the cheese. Whisk the egg whites until stiff and fold in.

Pour the filling over the biscuit base and chill in the refrigerator until firm. Carefully remove the cheesecake from the tin and place on a serving plate. Decorate with the fromage frais and fresh raspberries.

St Valentines

I invented these impressive hearts for our fourteenth wedding anniversary romantic dinner – they were delicious. I must admit that I am an incurable romantic and the theme of the dinner was hearts. We had a heart-shaped mousse for the starter and a heart-shaped filo pie for the main course! Our home is always full of hearts of one kind or another.

Ingredients: Imperial/Metric

8oz/225g	low fat cream cheese
5oz/150g	Greek strained yoghurt
1tbsp	honey
1	egg white
9oz/250g	raspberries

Richard Proof

Serves:	6
Calories:	57
Preparation Time:	30 minutes
Chilling Time:	4 hours

Garnish:

12	raspberries
6	variegated geranium leaves

Method:

1 Mix together the soft cheese, yoghurt and honey.

2 Whisk the egg white until stiff and fold into the cheese mixture.

3 Line 6 heart-shaped ceramic moulds (the ones with holes in their base) with muslin and spoon in the cheese mixture.

4 Place on a plate and leave to drain in the refrigerator for 4 hours.

5 Make the raspberry sauce by pressing the raspberries through a sieve and retaining their juices. Chill.

6 Turn out the moulds onto serving plates and pour the juice carefully around the hearts. Arrange the raspberries and geranium leaves to one side – being careful to maintain their heart shapes of course!

Pot Pourri

A pale cheesecake with subtle flavours that mingle together to make a mouth-watering dessert. The lavender not only looks stunning with the lemon colours but also smells delightful – just like an old-fashioned summer. Elderflowers and gooseberries are used together quite often in wine-making, as the flavours complement each other so well – this is merely an extension of that idea. Fortunately, my elderflower cheesecake tastes much better than Richard's elderflower wine!

Ingredients: Imperial/Metric

3	wholewheat cereal biscuits, crushed
1tbsp	honey
1	lemon (zest)
8oz/250g	gooseberries, washed, topped and tailed
3	heads of elder-flower
1tbsp	honey
1	lemon (zest and juice)
8oz/225g	low fat soft cheese
6fl oz/175ml	firm silken tofu, liquidized
2tbsp	sugar-free lemon marmalade
1oz/25g	gelatin

Richard Proof

Serves:	8
Calories:	113
Preparation Time:	40 minutes
Cooking Time:	5 minutes
Chilling Time:	2 hours
Oven Temperature:	190°C, 375°F, Gas Mark 5

Can be frozen

Garnish:

8	lemon twists
5oz/150g	low fat set yoghurt
1	small head of elder-flower, divided into 8
8	fresh lavender sprigs

Method:

1 Melt the honey and add to the crushed biscuits and lemon zest. Press into the bases of eight ramekin dishes. Bake for 5 minutes and leave to cool.
2 Place the gooseberries and honey in a pan. Tie the elderflowers in a piece of muslin and place in the pan. Cover and simmer for about 10 minutes. Allow to cool, remove the elderflowers, and then liquidize until smooth.
3 Place the soft cheese and tofu in a bowl and beat in the marmalade.
4 Mix the lemon juice and zest into the the gooseberry purée and stir into the cheese mixture.

5 Dissolve the gelatin in 2 tablespoons of boiling water. Leave to cool slightly before adding to the cheese mixture. Mix in thoroughly.

6 Spoon into the cake tin and smooth the surface. Leave to set in the refrigerator for 2 hours.

7 Garnish with the lemon twists, elderflower, lavender and yoghurt.

TIP BOX

To crush biscuits quickly and avoid a mess, place them in a plastic bag and crush with a rolling pin.

Oat Cuisine

The bright red of the strawberry looks lovely set against the orange of the mango. The high-fibre base has a nice nutty taste which complements the perfumed mango beautifully. This is a cheesecake which looks and tastes in a class of its own. I love experimenting with various kinds of garnish and this particular one is my favourite. The cheesecake actually looks far too nice to eat – Richard doesn't agree!

Ingredients: Imperial/Metric

2oz/50g	toasted whole-meal breadcrumbs
1oz/25g	oats
2	wholewheat cereal biscuits
2tbsp	honey
$\frac{1}{2}$tsp	vanilla essence
1	small mango, chopped
8oz/225g	ricotta cheese
10fl oz/250ml	*fromage frais*
2oz/50g	strawberries, washed and chopped
1pkt	sugar-free straw-berry jelly
4fl oz/125ml	boiling water
4oz/125g	strawberries

Richard Proof

Serves:	10
Calories:	97
Preparation Time:	45 minutes
Chilling Time:	5 hours
Cooking Time:	20 minutes
Oven Temperature:	160°C, 325°F, Gas Mark 3

Can be frozen

Garnish:

1pkt	sugar-free strawberry jelly
2	fresh lavender sprigs
2	red and white variegated geranium flowers
1	small sprig elderflower
4	orange wings

Method:

1   For the base, mix the first five ingredients together and press firmly into the base of an 8 in./20cm loose-bottomed cake tin. Bake for 20 minutes.
2   Make the jelly with 4fl oz/125ml water and leave to cool slightly.
3   Mix the ricotta cheese and *fromage frais* together.
4   Add the strawberries and mango.
5   Add the jelly slowly, mixing well.
6   Spoon onto the base and leave to set for 3 hours.
7   Scatter the strawberries on top of the cheesecake and make up the jelly as in 2 above. Leave to cool.
8   Pour the jelly onto the cheesecake and allow to set for 2 hours.
9   Make an attractive arrangement in the centre of the cheesecake with the various flowers and orange wings.

TIP BOX
Most cheesecakes freeze well. Best results are obtained if the cheesecake is frozen without its topping.

Chapter Seven
Filo Fantasies

Filo, or strudel pastry as it is sometimes called, doesn't seem to be used much in this country. We mainly associate this very thin, lace-like, pastry with Austrian apple strudel and believe, mistakenly, that this is all you can make with it. This couldn't be further from the truth. Filo pastry is very versatile and you can mould and sculpt it into different unusual shapes. A good friend of mine once made little filo 'frying pans' to serve vegetables in at a dinner party – very avant garde! You don't have to go to those lengths but it does show just how versatile filo is. You can make filo 'shells' which, when cooked, you fill with fruit, mousses, ice creams or sorbets. Unique little shapes which are guaranteed to pinch the limelight – whatever the occasion. The Greeks, who specialise in filo desserts, bake the filo and its filling together which gives a totally different effect. Whatever you decide upon, and there are lots of ideas in this chapter, I'm sure you will enjoy the experience.

I was introduced to filo pastry a good few years ago by some Greek friends of ours in Athens. Poppy, the female head of this extended family, made a traditional Greek dessert for us called Baklava. Although exceptionally sweet and heavily laden with sugar syrup I did eat quite a large piece. I was intrigued by all the very thin layers of pastry. I must have eaten a year's supply of sugar in that one dessert. Great pride is taken by the Greeks in their desserts and most women still make their own filo pastry by hand. What a laborious task that is! The filo leaves have to be thin enough to be able to read a newspaper through them. That's according to dear old Poppy – and I know from experience that it's true. Because I showed an interest in filo pastry I was paid the great honour of being invited to a family filo day. That's where all the female members of the family get together and make filo for the day. What an experience that was. I was fascinated by the whole process. The pastry is rolled out and then the women place their hands under it and begin to stretch it outwards making the pastry thinner and thinner. If the filo looks as though its going to tear then a little oil is brushed onto it. Needless to say I was roped into having a go. I started out quite well – I think so anyway – but then disaster struck. Each time I thought the filo was thin enough I eagerly proclaimed I'd done it. I was told in no uncertain terms that you couldn't read anything though my filo. I would keep on stretching, gingerly, and then my hand would burst throught the filo creating large holes. The Greek women laughed and laughed at my feeble efforts.

Luckily we don't have to spend hours and hours in the kitchen stretching our filo – we can buy it from the shops. I find that it is better to buy this pastry frozen from a supermarket. You can then store it for a couple of months and refreeze any leaves that remain unused. Fresh filo is available from some health shops and delicatessens but my experience with this type hasn't been good. On more than one occasion I have unwrapped the filo at home only to find it covered with green mould. Now I tend to buy filo from good supermarkets that have a rapid turnover. You do have to handle filo carefully and quickly but once you become used to it there's no problem. In order to ensure crispy layers that remain separate when cooked you need to brush each layer with a little oil. The beauty about filo pastry is that because the leaves are so very thin the fat and calorific content are far less than the pastry we are more familiar with in this country. In fact filo pastry contains only 275 calories per 100 grams and the fat content is a mere 4.2 grams – and of that, only 0.8 grams is saturated. That isn't bad at all for pastry is it?

Cashbags

A really sophisticated-looking dessert which is very easy to make. When I serve this at Harrow Ings the guests are always speculating on what exactly it is. Very soon this dessert becomes the centre of attention. Richard calls it a 'cashbag' because it looks like the bags of money that bank robbers held in the old movies.

Ingredients: Imperial/Metric

4	filo sheets
2oz/50g	dried prunes, pitted
2oz/50g	dried dates
2oz/50g	dried apricots
1tsp	ground cinnamon
2oz/50g	breadcrumbs
1tbsp	sesame seed oil

Richard Proof

Serves:	4
Calories:	158
Preparation Time:	30 minutes
Cooking Time:	25 minutes
Oven Temperature:	200°C, 400°F, Gas Mark 6

Can be frozen

Method:
1. Place the washed and dried fruit in a small pan with enough water to just cover the fruit. Simmer for about 10 minutes – until the fruit is plump.
2. Mix the breadcrumbs and cinnamon with the fruit and leave to one side.
3. Lightly oil the filo sheets and fold each in half, widthways.
4. Place a tablespoon of the fruit mixture in the centre of each filo.
5. Gather each corner and edge of the filo and draw over the fruit. Nip together at the top of the fruit and twist gently to form a cashbag.
6. Place on a lightly greased baking tray and cook for about 20 minutes until golden in colour.

> **TIP BOX**
> Once filo pastry has thawed you must keep it moist by placing a damp towel over the sheets not in use.

Arabian Nights

These little filo delights remind me of the hats they wore in the film *The Arabian Nights* – they are exactly the same shape.

Ingredients: Imperial/Metric

4	filo sheets
2oz/50g	strawberries, hulled
2oz/50g	bilberries
2oz/50g	redcurrants
2oz/50g	greengages, stoned
2tbsp	honey
1tbsp	sesame seed oil

Richard Proof

Serves:	4
Calories:	140
Preparation Time:	30 minutes
Cooking Time:	30 minutes
Oven Temperature:	200°C, 400°F, Gas Mark 6

Can be frozen

Method:

1 Place the washed fruit in a pan with the honey and heat gently for 5 minutes – just until the juices begin to run.
2 Divide each filo sheet into four equal quarters and brush each very lightly with oil.
3 Line four small, shallow dishes with the filo, using two squares for each dish. Don't trim the edges but leave the filo overlapping the dish.
4 Equally divide the fruit mixture between the dishes.
5 Using the two squares of filo for each dish, place the filo over the fruit mixture.
6 What we're going to do now is to make a kind of rope effect around the perimeter of the dish by gathering up the surplus filo and twisting it up onto the edge of the dish. Continue the entire way around until all the filo has been used.
7 Bake until lightly golden and serve warm.

Pillow Talk

Once you break into these lovely peach and strawberry pillows, the bright colours spill out and the effect is stunning. You can use any fruit inside these little filo pillows but I think that bright colours look the most effective.

Ingredients: Imperial/Metric

4	filo sheets
2	peaches, skinned and stoned
8oz/225g	strawberries, hulled
3oz/75g	wholemeal bread-crumbs
1tsp	freshly grated nutmeg
1tbsp	sesame oil

Richard Proof

Serves:	4
Calories:	145
Preparation Time:	30 minutes
Cooking Time:	20 minutes
Oven Temperature:	200°C, 400°F, Gas Mark 6

Can be frozen

Method:

1 Finely chop the peaches and halve the strawberries – larger ones may need quartering.
2 Mix the nutmeg and breadcrumbs with the fruit.
3 Lightly oil the filo sheets and fold each in half, widthways.
4 Spoon a tablespoon of the filling into the centre of each filo sheet.
5 Fold over the sides and edges to make a pillow shape.
6 Place on a lightly oiled baking sheet and bake until golden.

Catherine Wheels

The spiral shape of this filo dessert looks just like a Catherine wheel firework – hence the name. A beautifully subtle-flavoured filling that is naturally sweet with a hint of spice makes a lovely combination – an impressive end to any meal.

Ingredients: Imperial/Metric

4	filo sheets
2	bananas, ripe
1oz/25g	slivered almonds
$^1/_2$tsp	ground ginger
1tbsp	sesame seed oil

Garnish:
1tsp   ground ginger

Not Richard Proof
Poor Richard couldn't make the spiral shape because he stuffed too much filling inside. It just kept bursting open.

Serves:	4
Calories:	147
Preparation Time:	20 minutes
Cooking Time:	20 minutes
Oven Temperature:	200°C, 400°F, Gas Mark 6

Can be frozen

Method

1 Mash the banana well and add the ginger and almonds.
2 Lightly oil the filo sheets.
3 Divide the mixture into four equal portions.
4 Carefully place a quarter of the mixture along the long side of each filo sheet. The mixture should look like a long, firm sausage. Leave 1 in./2.5cm clear at both edges.
5 Carefully roll the filo sheet up, covering and recovering the banana mixture.
6 Starting with one end continue to spiral the tube around itself making a Catherine wheel effect.
7 Place on a baking sheet which has been lightly oiled and bake for about 20 minutes. Sprinkle with the ground ginger to garnish.

TIP BOX
Never thaw filo for longer than 2 hours as it will become unmanageable.

Swap Shop
Old Hat

This rich pastry dish is a favourite traditional dessert. By adding dates you not only sweeten naturally, but cut down calories as well! A guaranteed winner for a cold winter evening.

Richard Proof
Preparation Time: 30 minutes
Oven Temperature: 180°C, 350°F, Gas Mark 4

Serves: 6
Cooking Time: 30 minutes

Can be frozen

Traditional version

Healthier version

Calories: 230

Calories: 140

Ingredients: Imperial/Metric

2	filo sheets
1lb/450g	cooking apples, peeled and cored
4oz/100g	sugar
2oz/50g	sultanas
4oz/100g	breadcrumbs
1tsp	cinnamon
2oz/50g	butter, melted

Ingredients: Imperial/Metric

2	filo sheets
1lb/450g	cooking apples, peeled and cored
2oz/50g	dried dates, pitted
2oz/50g	sultanas
4oz/100g	wholemeal breadcrumbs
1tsp	cinnamon
1tbsp	sesame seed oil

Method:
Place the dried dates in a small saucepan and just cover with water. Simmer gently for about five minutes until the dates are soft and pulpy. Leave to cool. Chop the apple. Mix together the dates, apples, breadcrumbs, sultanas and cinnamon.

Lightly oil 2 sheets of filo and place one on top of the other.

Place a little of the filling near one edge, fold over the two sides and roll up. Repeat with the remaining filling – making sure that you finish with filo pastry on the top. Place on a lightly oiled baking sheet and bake until golden.

Mrs Miniver

The colours of this dessert are subtle and remind me of the delicate shade of the pink roses we have in our garden. Greer Garson, in the film *Mrs Miniver*, had a rose named after her – hence the name of this dessert. The delicate layers of filo surrounding the pale pink of the creamy filling looks elegant and sophisticated.

Ingredients: Imperial/Metric

4	filo sheets
4oz/125g	strawberries, hulled
7fl oz/200ml	*fromage frais*
1/₂oz/11g	gelatin
1tbsp	boiling water

Richard Proof:

Serves:	6
Calories:	50
Preparation Time:	30 minutes
Cooking Time:	15 minutes
Chilling Time:	1 hour
Oven Temperature:	200°C, 400°F, Gas Mark 6

Can be frozen

Garnish:
9   strawberry fans

Method:

1   Carefully line an 8 in./20cm tart tin with the filo pastry, brushing each sheet with a little oil.
2   Place the strawberries in a liquidizer with 2 tablespoons of the *fromage frais*. Blend until smooth.
3   Mix the remaining *fromage frais* with the strawberry mixture.
4   Dissolve the gelatin in the boiling water and add to the *fromage* mixture.
5   Pour this mixture into the baked filo tart and leave to set in the refrigerator for about 1 hour.
6   Make strawberry fans without hulling the strawberries.
7   Arrange the strawberry fans around the edge of the dessert, and serve chilled.

TIP BOX

Buy filo from a reputable shop with a quick turnover. Once filo becomes a little aged, after a few months, it becomes brittle and impossible to handle.

A Star is Born

This is a most attractive dessert which you can make with any fruits you wish. I like using exotic fruits as they look a little bit different and have such a nice aroma. The effect of these little delights is absolutely stunning.

Ingredients: Imperial/Metric

2	filo sheets
2	passion fruit
1	star fruit, washed
2oz/50g	kumquats, washed
2oz/50g	ripe cherries, washed

Richard Proof

Serves:	4
Calories:	53
Preparation Time:	15 minutes
Cooking Time:	15 minutes
Oven Temperature:	200°C, 400°F, Gas Mark 6

Can be frozen

Garnish:

4   sprigs of mint

Method:

1   Cut each of the filo sheets into four quarters and oil lightly. Fold each in half.
2   Carefully line four fluted brioche tins, using 2 quarters for each one.
3   Bake in the oven for 15 minutes until golden and crisp.
4   Leave to cool slightly before very carefully lifting out of the tins – the pastry at this stage is very brittle and delicate.
5   Scoop the flesh and seeds from the passion fruit.
6   Slice the star fruit thinly.
7   Cut the cherries in half and remove the stones.
8   Slice the kumquats or, if they are really small, leave them whole.
9   Arrange the fruit in the 'shells' of filo and garnish with the mint.

TIP BOX

For a nice change, why not coat the brioche cases in carob chocolate. A tasty layer of carob enveloping crispy filo pastry – what an irresistible thought.

Swap Shop
Bougatsa

Some very dear Greek friends of ours introduced Richard and me to this dessert many years ago when we were in Crete. Traditionally it's very, very sweet – as most Greek desserts are – but can be made healthier quite easily. I always think of Greece when I eat this beautiful filo delight.

Not Richard Proof
Somehow Richard managed to make the semolina very lumpy which really spoilt the smooth nature of this base. What made it worse was that he didn't own up until we were eating it – by which time the semolina lumps had been transformed into small bullets . . . .

Serves: 8 *Preparation Time*: 30 minutes *Cooking Time*: 25 minutes
Oven Temperature: 190°C, 375°F, Gas Mark 5 *Can be frozen*

Traditional version | *Healthier version*

Calories: 220 | Calories: 108

Ingredients: Imperial/Metric		**Ingredients:** Imperial/Metric	
4oz/100g	semolina	4oz/100g	wholemeal semolina
10fl oz/250ml	full cream milk	10fl oz/250ml	skimmed milk
4oz/100g	sugar	2tbsp	honey
3	eggs	2	egg whites
$\frac{1}{2}$tsp	vanilla essence	$\frac{1}{2}$tsp	vanilla essence
8	filo sheets	8	filo sheets
2oz/50g	butter, melted	1tbsp	sesame seed oil
2tsp	cinnamon	2tsp	cinnamon

Method:

In a heavy-based saucepan mix the semolina, milk, honey and egg whites. Stir continuously over a gentle heat until the mixture becomes thick. I find that a balloon whisk is ideal for this.

Remove from the heat, stir in the vanilla essence. Cover with non-PVC cling film and leave to go cold.

Lightly oil a filo sheet and fold in half, widthways. Place about 3 tablespoons of the mixture along one narrow edge about 2 in./5cm from the base and sides. Carefully fold the bottom edge of the filo loosely over the filling. Fold in the sides.

Roll up loosely to the end of the filo sheet and place on a baking sheet – join side down.

Repeat with the remaining ingredients.

Lightly brush the tops with oil. Bake for about 25 minutes until golden. Sprinkle with cinnamon to serve.

Marron

Unlike most nuts, chestnuts are very low in fat and have a much higher starch content. Their presence in human diets has been dated back to prehistoric times and they were probably a staple food of early hunter gatherers. The chestnut and coffee combination make this rich pastry an unusual and rich treat.

Ingredients: Imperial/Metric

8	filo sheets
1tbsp	sesame seed oil
1tbsp	decaffeinated coffee
1tbsp	boiling water
6oz/125g	chestnut purée
6oz/125g	*fromage frais*
1tbsp	honey

Richard Proof

Serves:	8
Calories:	114
Preparation Time:	15 minutes
Cooking Time:	20 minutes
Oven Temperature:	200°C, 400°F, Gas Mark 6

Can be frozen

Method:

1 Dissolve the coffee granules in the water. Leave to cool.
2 Place the chestnut purée, coffee, *fromage frais* and honey in a liquidizer and blend until smooth.
3 Lightly oil each of the filo sheets and lay four in the base of a shallow, oven-proof dish.
4 Place the chestnut mixture on the top and cover with the remaining four filo sheets. Tuck the edges of the filo under the top sheet.
5 Cook for about 20 minutes until golden.

King of Hearts

Raisins were mentioned in the Bible on a number of occasions and must have been considered quite important as King David accepted the fruit in lieu of taxes. These little heart shaped desserts look most impressive and are perfect for that special occasion. An added bonus is the fact that they are quick and easy to make.

Ingredients: Imperial/Metric

4	filo sheets
1oz/25g	raisins
6oz/175g	*fromage frais*
1tbsp	honey
1oz/25g	carob bar
½oz/11g	gelatin
1tbsp	boiling water
1tbsp	sesame seed oil

Richard Proof

Serves:	4
Calories:	190
Preparation Time:	15 minutes
Cooking Time:	15 minutes
Oven Temperature:	200°C, 400°F, Gas Mark 6

Can be frozen

Garnish:
4   carob fans
4   sprigs of mint

Method:
1   Brush each of the filo sheets with a little oil and cut each sheet into four quarters.
2   Carefully line four heart-shaped baking tins using four squares of filo for each one. Bake for 15 minutes.
3   Dissolve the gelatin in the boiling water.
4   Mix together the *fromage frais*, honey, raisins and gelatin.
5   Pour into the heart-shaped filo 'shells' and place in the refrigerator to set for about 30 minutes.
6   Break up the carob and place in a small bowl standing in a pan of hot water. Stir until the carob has melted.
7   Using a teaspoon, carefully drizzle the melted carob over the hearts making a zig-zag pattern. Serve garnished with mint sprigs and carob fans.

Chapter Eight
Frozen Assets

Ice creams, sorbets and ices are loved by everyone – adults and children alike. And, the beauty about them is that they are extremely quick and easy to make. Even Richard can make them without experiencing any difficulty whatsoever.

The variety of these frozen assets is endless. You could eat a different one each day of the year and never repeat a flavour. The whole spectrum of fresh and dried fruit is at your disposal. I tend to use the fresh fruit that is in surplus supply on the local market stall, when the prices are rock bottom. The many redcurrant, blackcurrant and gooseberry bushes in our garden are harvested with relish each summer and turned into the most delightful frozen desserts. In the cold depths of winter, it's lovely to eat desserts that were made and frozen in the height of summer. The memories of the warm sun on your back and the ripe, plump fruit waiting to be picked all come flooding back.

The fruit you use can be mixed and matched in any combination you fancy. The concoctions you can come up with are incredible. Like my 'Surprise Delight' recipe, for example. What strange bedfellows prunes and brown bread make. People are always a little reluctant to try that dessert – but only if you tell them what's in it before they taste it. Just keep it a secret until their glasses are clean and then surprise them. It's a wonderfully different ice cream where the combination of textures and flavours works very well indeed. Should you tire of fruity-tasting ices, then you can always turn to spices, herbs, carob and coffee to tempt the old taste buds.

Ice cream has a long and interesting history. It is thought to have originated in the Far East and from there the Italians imported the idea and it rapidly spread throughout the rest of Europe. In Britain, ice cream made its appearance in the seventeenth century, but it was a luxury – exclusively reserved for the rich. Special ice houses were built in the grounds of large country estates in order to keep the ice cream frozen. Deep pits were dug in the earth and were lined with bricks. A roof was built and then ice was collected from local lakes and ponds during winter and deposited in these ice houses.

Ice cream could then be enjoyed by the rich throughout the year. The first ice house was built by Charles II in the mid-seventeenth century, and thus it was considered 'the thing to have' at that time. You can see why ice cream was described as 'eating winter with a spoon', can't you? What an apt saying! Thank goodness we don't have to go to those lengths to keep ice cream cold today.

The problem with 'traditional' ice cream is that it contains an abundance of saturated fat, cholesterol, sugar and calories. It's all that cream, sugar and egg yolks that do it. Homemade ice cream is often thought of as being good for you as it contains 'natural' ingredients. The fact remains, however, that it is a cholesterol cocktail and should be avoided if it is made according to 'traditional' recipes. And the commercial varieties have so many additives, colourings and flavourings that you don't really know what you're eating. Would you believe that a report compiled a couple of years ago found that a certain make of ice cream used pork fat as its main ingredient? What a worrying thought that is.

Anyway, you can enjoy ice cream without any worries at all if you slightly adapt your recipes. To replace the cream I often use yoghurt or tofu and I use honey or fruit juice, instead of sugar. The taste and texture remains virtually the same but the 'baddies' have done a disappearing act. You are left with a tasty ice cream that is actually good for you – and won't increase your padding.

Richard's father used to make ice cream and he was the first person to sell it at the Darwen Cricket Club in Lancashire during the mid-1930s. Richard remembers him pushing his hand-made cart around the ground selling his wares. Any ice cream left at the end of the day was shared out amongst the children – no wonder Richard loves ice cream.

Sorbets are very refreshing and are much lighter than ice creams. I love to eat a fresh-fruit sorbet piled into a tall, elegant glass when I can manage to snatch a minute to relax in the garden on a warm sunny day. And, unfortunately, that doesn't happen very often these days. Sorbets are traditionally made with lots of sugar which is added to fruit and egg whites. The sugar is easily replaced with fruit juices and honey to give you a healthier sorbet. As with ice cream, the variety is endless and the combinations know no boundaries. It's really good fun experimenting with the different colours and textures and children love it.

If you like a really creamy-textured ice cream or smooth sorbet then simply keep liquidizing the mixture and refreezing it. this helps to break down the ice particles thus making the mixture smoother. Personally I prefer the ice particles to give an extra texture to the dessert. But tastes do differ – Richard prefers it smooth!

The Medicine Tree

The papaya plant has such strong legendary healing powers associated with it that in many parts of Africa and the Caribbean it is called 'the medicine tree'. This is a lovely pale-coloured sorbet with a subtle flavour. It looks and tastes wonderful.

Ingredients: Imperial/Metric

2	ripe papaya
1tbsp	honey
3tbsp	fresh lime juice
2	egg whites

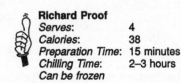

Richard Proof
Serves: 4
Calories: 38
Preparation Time: 15 minutes
Chilling Time: 2–3 hours
Can be frozen

86

Method:

1 Purée the papaya in a liquidizer.

2 Add the honey and lime juice and blend until smooth.

3 Whisk the egg whites until stiff and carefully fold into the mixture.

4 Follow steps 3 to 5 for 'New Zealand Sunset' on page 88.

TIP BOX

Always leave at least 1 in./2.5cm at the top of the freezer container when freezing liquids as they expand and force the lid off.

Swap Shop Recipe
Frosty the Snowman

This creamy mint-chocolate ice cream is deceptively rich – and at less than one-quarter of the calories of traditional ice cream, you can enjoy it more often!

Richard Proof
Serves: 10   *Preparation Time*: 15 minutes   *Chilling Time*: 3 hours
Can be frozen

Traditional version

Healthier version

Calories: 176

Calories: 37

Ingredients: Imperial/Metric

11fl oz/300ml	double cream
1fl oz/30ml	full cream milk
3oz/75g	plain chocolate
1tbsp	freshly chopped mint

Ingredients: Imperial/Metric

11fl oz/300ml	firm silken tofu
1fl oz/30ml	skimmed milk
3oz/75g	sugar-free carob bar
1tbsp	freshly chopped mint

Method:

Line a 1¹/₂pt/600ml basin with cling film.

Liquidize the tofu and milk together.

Break the carob into small pieces and place in a bowl over a pan of boiling water. Stir occasionally until melted.

Swirl the melted carob and mint through the tofu mixture.

Pour into the lined basin and freeze.

Simply unmould the 'frost' and serve on an attractive plate.

New Zealand Sunset

The kiwi fruit is grown predominantly in New Zealand. This delicately flavoured sorbet is wonderfully refreshing – especially on a hot summer day. For a change you could add some fresh mint from the garden.

Ingredients:

6	kiwi fruit
1	lemon (zest and juice)
1tbsp	honey

Richard Proof

Serves:	4
Calories:	45
Preparation Time:	10 minutes
Chilling Time:	2–3 hours
Can be frozen	

Method:

1 Purée the kiwi fruit in a liquidizer.
2 Add the remaining ingredients and blend until smooth.
3 Pour into a shallow freezer container and freeze for 1–2 hours, until solid around the edges.
4 Beat with an electric mixer until the mixture is smooth.
5 Cover and refreeze for 1 hour.

The Policeman's Helmet

Ice cream *bombes* remind me of two things – a policeman's helmet and the archways of a church. I do, however, have rather a vivid imagination – as Richard is always reminding me. Ice cream *bombes* are most impressive and are ideal for that special occasion when you want something a little different. Each time I make one it becomes the centre of the conversation and everyone wants to learn the recipe. They are also wonderful at parties and children go wild over them.

The thing to remember about *bombes* is that they are made up of different layers – usually three – so it's important to consider the flavours and the colours. You can choose contrasting colours to give a striking visual effect, such as the 'Cassis', 'Soft and Silky' and 'Frosty the Snowman', or choose colours that only subtly change such as 'Tenerife Temptation', 'Surprise Delight' and 'Soft and Silky'. Whichever you decide upon I'm sure that you will make a *bombe* more than once.

Although *bombes* look quite difficult and time consuming to make, they are, in fact, very easy to prepare. All you have to do is choose the three ice cream flavours you want and make up as outlined by the recipes. When the ice creams are firm, not frozen, pack a layer of one flavour tightly around the edge of a mould. (I tend to use an ordinary basin.) Place the mould in the freezer until the first layer is frozen. Do exactly the same thing with the next layer of ice cream, leaving a hollow in the centre. This hollow is then filled with the third and final layer and frozen until solid. Unmould and serve.

You can if you like make *mini-bombes* by using small moulds such as timbale or ramekin dishes. And, to be a little different, you could pack fresh fruit into the centre and freeze. They are such fun to make and to eat that you can experiment with a number of different ideas.

Surprise Delight

I know what you're thinking, 'She's gone too far this time, hasn't she?' Well I must admit that when I served this up to Richard for the first time and told him what was in it he was, to say the least, reluctant to even try it. And that, for this ice cream addict, was something. Anyway, curiosity got the better of him and he tucked in. Surprise, surprise – he loved it. Now this creamy dessert has become a regular on the menu of 'Harrow Ings' and everyone loves it.

Ingredients: Imperial/Metric

8oz/225g	dried prunes
15fl oz/400ml	soft silken tofu, liquidized
4fl oz/125ml	low fat natural yoghurt
3	egg whites
3oz/75g	wholemeal bread-crumbs, toasted

Richard Proof

Serves: 8
Calories: 82
Preparation Time: 30 minutes
Chilling Time: 3 hours
Can be frozen

Method:

1 Place the prunes in a pan with just enough water to cover and simmer for about 10 minutes. The prunes should be soft and pulpy. Leave to cool and then liquidize.

2 Place the tofu, yoghurt, breadcrumbs and prunes in a basin.

3 Whisk the egg whites until stiff and carefully fold into the mixture.

4 Pour into a shallow freezer container and freeze for about an hour. It should be just on the point of freezing.

5 Liquidize the frozen mixture and refreeze in a container that is big enough to take scoops from.

Bangkok Beauty

I love the perfumed quality of the mango. Everything you make with it has such a wonderful aroma. The stone of the mango is large and flat so it's always best to peel the mango and then slice the fruit from the stone. Richard and I always fight over who 'cleans' the stone! This sorbet is simple to make and truly refreshing – not to mention nourishing!

Ingredients:

2	ripe mangoes
1tbsp	honey
2	oranges (zest and juice)
2	egg whites

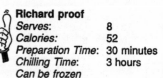

Richard Proof
Serves: 4
Calories: 45
Preparation Time: 15 minutes
Chilling Time: 2–3 hours
Can be frozen

Method:
1 Peel and chop the mango flesh.
2 Place in a liquidizer with the honey and orange zest and juice.
3 Blend until smooth.
4 Whisk the egg whites until stiff and fold into the mixture.
5 Follow steps 3 to 5 for 'New Zealand Sunset' on page 88.

Soft and Silky

This is probably my favourite ice cream. The addition of the ginger gives the flavour a real boost and contrasts exceptionally well with the subtle peach. I seem to add ginger to most things these days – it's a good job that it's good for me!

Ingredients: Imperial/Metric

4	fresh peaches, skinned
11fl oz/300ml	soft silken tofu, liquidized
5fl oz/150ml	Greek strained yoghurt
2	egg whites
2tsp	green ginger wine
2	pieces of stem ginger, chopped
1tbsp	honey

Richard proof
Serves: 8
Calories: 52
Preparation Time: 30 minutes
Chilling Time: 3 hours
Can be frozen

From top left: a creamy cheesecake, Bali Sunrise; Jolly Jesters (jellies containing only 31 calories); a kiwi sorbet, New Zealand Sunset; King of Hearts (pastry filled with raisins and *fromage frais*, topped with carob), and Jolly Miner, a pudding with gooseberries and apple

A subtle peach ice cream, Soft and Silky, is shown on the left next to the baked cheesecake, Solomon's Nectar, and the colourful Hippocrates, a combination of papaya, lychees and kumquats

Huckleberry Finn — a delicious bilberry cheesecake that's low in calories and high on taste

Clockwise from back left: a steamed apple pudding, Scarb Jacket; in the background, a rich brown bread ice cream, Surprise Delight; a delicate fruit salad, My Darling Clementine, and Pozo, an apple tart topped with fresh raspberries on a low-fat pastry base

From left to right: Blackberry and apple laced with blackcurrant *crème de cassis* form the layered Apple Johns; the fruit-filled Days of Wine and Roses is a healthy version of Summer Pudding, and Passion, a fool made with passion fruit

From left to right: Shades of Summer, a delicate strawberry ice cream; Party Piece (low-sugar meringue, frozen *fromage frais*, ginger and low-fat ice cream), and St Valentines served with two sauces, Apollo (made with orange) and Red Zinger (raspberry and apple)

Mistral, an unusual variation on a cheesecake, looks dramatic with its contrasting colours and textures (cheese and fig) encased in a French stick. In the far right corner you can just see Striped Sensation, a colourful combination of yoghurt, banana and carob, in stemmed glasses

From left to right: Tenerife Temptation, a rich banana ice cream; the blackberry and peach cobbler, Roman Ruin, and the fruit extravaganza, Archangel's wings

This appropriately named fruit salad, Exotica, looks spectacular with its bright contrasting colours and unusual shapes. A real treat for the senses

Lychees, kumquats, passion fruit and star fruit form the basis of Bishop's Mitres in the foreground, with Tops and Tails (a blackcurrant and orange pie) in the centre; the Blushing Brides (easy-to-make strawberry fools) are to the left

Limey, a refreshing tangy mousse, is pictured top left and bottom right, with the watermelon sorbet, Red Ice, and cherry pudding, Ait-Skeiters

Hades and Minthe is a mouthwatering mint and carob 'chocolate' cheesecake which looks elegant moulded into a heart

A classical French apple tart is transformed into the impressive 'Allo 'Allo. Deep pink Cassis ice cream, on the right, looks best served in glasses

From left to right: Wagon Wheel (a tasty combination of carob and *fromage frais*), served with a rich vanilla sauce, Climbing Orchid; the pretty Mrs Miniver, consisting of layers of filo surrounding a strawberry cream, and in the background, the rich carob and banana mousse, St John's Bread

Method:

1 Chop the peaches and place in the liquidizer with the tofu, yoghurt, green ginger wine and honey.
2 Blend until smooth.
3 Whisk the egg whites until stiff.
4 Stir the chopped stem ginger into the tofu mixture and gently fold in the egg whites.
5 Pour into a shallow freezer container and freeze until the edges are frozen but the middle is still fairly soft.
6 Break up and liquidize.
7 Refreeze in a container that is deep enough to take scoops from.

Cassis

Any berries can be used in this recipe and the result will always be superb. It's a tasty ice cream that is quite high in fibre because of the fruit seeds present.

Ingredients: Imperial/Metric

8oz/225g	blackberries
8oz/225g	raspberries
8oz/225g	cooking apples
5fl oz/150ml	Greek strained yoghurt
5fl oz/150ml	soft silken tofu, liquidized
2	egg whites

Richard Proof
Serves: 8
Calories: 47
Preparation Time: 25 minutes
Chilling Time: 3 hours
Can be frozen

Method:

1 Wash the fruit and pick over them carefully.
2 Place in a covered pan with the chopped apple and cook gently for about 10 minutes.
3 Cool and liquidize.
4 Stir in the yoghurt and tofu and pour into a shallow tray. Freeze for 1 hour.
5 Whisk the egg whites until stiff.
6 Place the berry mixture in the liquidizer and blend. Pour into a bowl and gradually and carefully fold in the egg whites.
7 Pour into a freezer container and freeze.

TIP BOX

For a ripple effect in the ice cream, all you do is alternate layers of ice cream and fruit purée. When you scoop out the ice cream you have a stunning striped pattern.

Iced Dream

Richard loves ice cream. He can eat any flavour at almost any time of the day! I must admit that I am not quite as keen. The colour of this ice cream is deep red – it looks beautiful.

Ingredients: Imperial/Metric

8oz/225g	raspberries, frozen
11fl oz/300ml	low fat natural yoghurt
2	egg whites

Richard Proof
Serves:	8
Calories:	28
Preparation Time:	10 minutes
Chilling Times:	3 hours
Can be frozen	

Method:
1 Place the raspberries and yoghurt into a liquidizer and blend until fairly smooth.
2 Pour into a shallow freezer container and freeze for 1 hour.
3 Remove from the freezer, break up and liquidize.
4 Whisk the egg whites until stiff and fold into the mixture.
5 Refreeze in a deep container.

Red Ice

The rich, bright pink of the watermelon looks stunning in this subtly flavoured sorbet. A winner with everyone who tastes it.

Ingredients: Imperial/Metric

8oz/225g	watermelon flesh
1	orange (zest and juice)
1tbsp	honey
2	egg whites

Richard Proof
Serves:	4
Calories:	32
Preparation Time:	15 minutes
Chilling Time:	4 hours
Can be frozen	

Method:
1 Remove the seeds from the watermelon and purée the flesh in a liquidizer with the honey and orange juice and zest.
2 Pour the watermelon mixture into a shallow freezer container and freeze for 3 hours.
3 Purée in a blender until smooth.
4 Whisk the egg whites until stiff and carefully fold into the watermelon mixture.
5 Refreeze until firm.

Swap Shop Recipe
Tenerife Temptation

The nicest bananas I have ever tasted were in Tenerife. In fact, I spent most of our holiday visiting banana plantations and wolfing down handfuls of this fruit. The banana flavour of this ice cream is enhanced by a hint of lemon – deliciously refreshing.

Richard Proof
Serves: 8   *Preparation Time*: 20 minutes   *Chilling Time*: 4 hours
Can be frozen

Traditional version

Calories: 238

Ingredients: Imperial/Metric

14oz/400g	bananas
5fl oz/150ml	double cream
5fl oz/150ml	single cream
1	lemon (juice)
5oz/150g	sugar
2	egg whites

Healthier version

Calories: 69

Ingredients: Imperial/Metric

14oz/400g	bananas
5fl oz/150ml	soft silken tofu, liquidized
5fl oz/150ml	low fat natural yoghurt
1	lemon (juice)
1tbsp	honey
2	egg whites

Method:

Peel and mash the bananas in a bowl using a fork.

Add the tofu, yoghurt, lemon juice and honey. Beat well making sure that everything is combined.

Pour into a shallow freezer container and freeze until it looks mushy.

Whisk the egg whites until stiff and fold into the banana mixture.

Refreeze in a deep container for about 3 hours.

TIP BOX

If you plan to make a lot of ice cream, it might be worth investing in an ice cream maker. This will save you both time and effort.

Party Piece

This is a most stunning dessert – yet it is not too difficult to make. It's made up of low-sugar meringue and frozen *fromage frais* with pieces of ginger suspended in it – all encased in a rich creamy ice cream. Totally irresistible.

Ingredients: Imperial/Metric

1qty	'Sweetheart' base (see page 54)
¹/₂qty	'Tenerife Temptation' (see page 93)
10fl oz/275ml	*fromage frais*
2oz/50g	stem ginger, chopped

Richard Proof

Serves:	10
Calories:	74
Preparation Time:	40 minutes
Cooking Time:	60 minutes
Chilling Time:	3 hours
Oven Temperature:	150°C, 300°F, Gas Mark 2

Can be frozen

Garnish:

2oz/50g *fromage frais*

Method:

1   Put the meringue into a piping bag, fitted with a 1cm, plain nozzle. Carefully pipe 3 6 in./15cm rounds onto a baking sheet lined with greased, greaseproof paper. Bake for 1 hour. Peel off the paper and cool on a wire rack.
2   Remove the ice cream from the freezer and leave for 20 minutes at room temperature.
3   Fold the ginger into the *fromage frais*.
4   Line an 8 in./20cm cake tin with a layer of the ice cream – the layer should be about 1 in./2.5cm thick.
5   Place a meringue round on the top and cover with half of the fromage frais mixture. Repeat these layers and top with the third round of meringue. Any spaces at the sides should be filled with the ice cream.
6   Cover with foil and freeze for 3 hours.
7   Place in the refrigerator 1 hour before serving and turn out onto a serving plate. Garnish and serve.

Shades of Summer

The beautiful pale pink of this ice cream is broken by the bright red strawberry halves which are encapsulated within it. A wonderful treat for the taste buds which is best served solo – that way you really appreciate the flavour.

Ingredients: Imperial/Metric

1lb/450g	strawberries, washed and hulled
11fl oz/300ml	low fat natural yoghurt
2	egg whites

Richard Proof

Serves:	10
Calories:	31
Preparation Time:	20 minutes
Chilling Time:	3 hours
Can be frozen	

Method:

1. Place $^2/_3$lb/300g of the strawberries into a blender with the yoghurt. Blend until smooth.
2. Pour this mixture into a shallow freezer container and freeze for 1 hour.
3. Remove from the freezer, break up and liquidize.
4. Whisk the egg whites until stiff and carefully fold into the mixture.
5. Cut in half the remaining strawberries and drop into the mixture – stirring very gently.
6. Refreeze.

None of that boring stuff for me. I'll have apple pie!
I think I'll try a healthy sweet...
TRADITIONAL
APPLE PIE
sherry trifle
Black Forest gateau
HEALthy
Jolly Jesters
Pluto a Menth
Arabian Nights

Chapter Nine
The Proof Is In The Pudding

Puddings are an old British tradition and as far back as the seventeenth century, puddings like 'Sweet Gingerbread Man' and 'Staff of Life' were uniquely popular in this country and relatively unknown elsewhere in the world. Britain has, over the years, become famous for its good old 'puds'.

The current health trend towards fresh fruit and light desserts – and consequently away from puddings – could make the old British pudding a thing of the past. And that would be a great shame for a number of reasons. What many of the healthy eating preachers fail to realize is that you don't have to give up everything to eat properly. Puddings can be adapted into healthier versions, just like any other recipe.

The suet, which many of the older recipes contain in abundance, can easily be replaced with a healthier margarine and we can use fruit juices, honey and flavourful herbs to sweeten instead of sugar. By using wholemeal flour, wholemeal breadcrumbs, oats and fruit we are substantially increasing the fibre content. So from a health point of view, puddings certainly can be good for you – providing essential nutrients and fibre without the saturated fat, cholesterol and calories. It's a perfect compromise, isn't it?

Nothing is more heartening than eating a pudding on a bitterly cold winter's day when the snow is whistling around the house. It's nice to be snug and warm inside, eating a stodgy pudding. As my Mum would say, 'Puddings stick to your ribs and keep the cold out'.

Most puddings are relatively easy to make and fairly quick to prepare. Steamed puddings, however, can take over two hours to cook – and that's a long time for this busy world in which we live. The ideal short cut is to make use of a pressure cooker – it reduces the steaming period to just 30 minutes. Marvellous, isn't it? All you have to do is stand the pudding basin on the trivet and pour in about 750ml of boiling water. Make sure the pudding is tightly secured with a foil lid or else the moisture will make the pudding wet and soggy.

Place the lid on the pressure cooker and when the steam shoots through the top, pop the weight on. Steam for about 30 minutes. And there you have it – a steamed pud in minutes instead of hours. If you own a microwave you could 'steam' the puddings even more quickly. But remember not to use metal containers. 'Steamed' on full power in a microwave, a pudding should take about 10 minutes. Keep checking though – you could end up with a biscuit!

The Jolly Miner

Lancashire was reputed to grow the best gooseberries in the country. About a century ago, working men would grow gooseberries and enter them in the 'Gooseberry Show', in the hope of winning first prize for the heaviest berry. Quaint names were given to these prize gooseberries and they often reflected the grower's occupation. So names have been recorded like, 'The Jolly Miner', 'Lancashire Lad' and 'The Jolly Painter'. This pudding is particular tasty – with the unusual combination of gooseberries and apples.

Ingredients: Imperial/Metric

8oz/250g	gooseberries, washed
8oz/250g	cooking apples, washed
4fl oz/125ml	apple juice
2tsp	freshly grated nutmeg
8oz/225g	wholemeal flour
3tsp	low-sodium baking powder
4oz/100g	polyunsaturated, unhydrogenated margarine
1tsp	honey
5fl oz/150ml	skimmed milk

Not Richard Proof
Unfortunately, Richard didn't know what 'cream together' meant – he merely stirred it gently to combine the ingredients.

Serves:	8
Calories:	225
Preparation Time:	20 minutes
Cooking Time:	45 minutes
Oven Temperature:	180°C, 350°F, Gas Mark 4

Can be frozen

Method:

1 Top and tail the gooseberries, core the apples and slice them thinly.
2 Place the fruit and juice in the base of a 2pt/1.2 litre shallow, oven–proof dish. Sprinkle the grated nutmeg over the fruit.
3 Cream the margarine and honey together until the mixture is light and fluffy.
4 Sift the flour and baking powder into the mixture and gently fold until the ingredients are combined well. Carefully stir in the milk.
5 Spoon this mixture over the gooseberries and apples.
6 Bake for about 45 minutes, until the topping springs back when touched.

TIP BOX
Make sure you beat – preferably with an electric mixer – the honey and margarine. The mixture should be light and fluffy in texture.

Scarb Jackets

Apples were commonly called 'scarb jackets' in Anglo-Saxon times. You can only eat this pudding after a very light meal, it's so very filling. I like the apple grated because that way its flavour is spread throughout the whole pudding. If you prefer, you can chop the apple which will result in pockets of apple.

Ingredients: Imperial/Metric

4oz/125g	wholemeal flour
3tsp	low-sodium baking powder
2oz/50g	wholemeal bread-crumbs
3oz/75g	polyunsaturated, unhydrogenated margarine
4oz/125g	dessert apples, washed and grated
4oz/125g	dried dates, pitted
1	lemon (zest)
2fl oz/50ml	skimmed milk

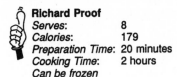

Richard Proof
Serves: 8
Calories: 179
Preparation Time: 20 minutes
Cooking Time: 2 hours
Can be frozen

Method:

1 Rub the margarine into the flour until it resembles fine breadcrumbs.
2 Add the breadcrumbs, apple and lemon zest.
3 Place the dates in a small pan with just enough water to cover, and simmer for about 5 minutes until they are soft and pulpy. Add to the flour mixture and stir well.
4 Make a well in the centre of the mixture and add enough milk to give a soft dropping consistency.
5 Spoon the mixture into a lightly greased 2pt/900ml pudding basin, cover with greased foil (pleated down the centre), and tie securely with string.
6 Steam for about 2 hours. Serve upturned on a plate.

Swap Shop Recipe
Christmas Cracker

Christmas just wouldn't be Christmas without a good old traditional pudding. Personally I will never understand how sugar managed to creep into such a naturally sweet dessert. This recipe has no added sugar and yet it tastes just as sweet as the 'normal' one!

Not Richard Proof
Richard forgot to add the breadcrumbs and so the pudding was very heavy and very moist – some might even say soggy!
Serves: 10   *Preparation Time*: 1hour
Cooking Time: 4 hours plus 3 hours before serving   *Can be frozen*

Traditional version		*Healthier version*	
Calories: 509		Calories: 391	
Ingredients: Imperial/Metric		**Ingredients:** Imperial/Metric	
8oz/225g	brown sugar	8oz/225g	dried dates
8oz/225g	shredded suet	8oz/225g	polyunsaturated unhydrogenated margarine
4oz/100g	currants	4oz/100g	currants
4oz/100g	sultanas	4oz/100g	sultanas
4oz/125g	candied peel	2	lemons (zest)
		2	oranges (zest)
4oz/125g	breadcrumbs	4oz/125g	wholemeal breadcrumbs
4oz/125g	plain flour	4oz/125g	wholemeal plain flour
4oz/100g	black treacle	1tbsp	black molasses
		1	lemon (juice)
5fl oz/150ml	rum	5fl oz/150ml	rum or skimmed milk
2	eggs	2	egg whites
3tsp	mixed spice	$\frac{1}{2}$tsp	ground ginger
		$\frac{1}{2}$tsp	grated nutmeg
		1tsp	ground cinnamon
		1tsp	mixed spice

Method:
Place the dates in a small saucepan with the rum and heat gently for about 5 minutes until soft and pulpy. Leave to cool slightly.
Cream together the dates and margarine. Beat in the egg whites, molasses, lemon juice and fruit zest.

Add all the remaining ingredients and stir well.

Place the mixture into a well greased 2pt/900ml pudding basin and cover with greased, greaseproof paper. Tie down well with string. Steam for 4 hours.

You will need to store the pudding in a cool dry place. Steam again for another 3 hours prior to serving.

Jolly Green Giant

This is, to say the least, an unusual pudding. For one thing, a vegetable is used as the main ingredient and, for another, it's predominantly green in colour. There is only one problem with this pudding – there is never enough of it. It's everyone's favourite.

Ingredients: Imperial/Metric

8oz/225g	courgettes, washed
6oz/176g	wholemeal flour
1tbsp	honey
3tsp	low-sodium baking powder
4oz/125g	polyunsaturated, unhydrogenated margarine
2oz/50g	sultanas
2tsp	green ginger wine
1oz/25g	stem ginger, chopped finely
1tsp	ground ginger
1tbsp	skimmed milk

Richard Proof

Serves:	8
Calories:	225
Preparation Time:	20 minutes
Cooking Time:	45 minutes
Oven Temperature:	180°C, 350°F, Gas Mark 4

Can be frozen

Method:

1. Beat together the honey and margarine until the mixture is light and fluffy.
2. Grate the courgettes and add them to the mixture with the chopped stem ginger, sultanas, ginger wine and milk. Do not stir.
3. Sift the flour, baking powder and ground ginger into the mixture and stir gently.
4. Spoon the mixture into a lightly greased 7in./18cm square baking tin.
5. Cook for about 45 minutes until the pudding feels springy to the touch.
6. Cut into squares and serve hot.

TIP BOX

You can also make individual puddings by spooning the mixture into small metal pudding basins. Reduce the cooking time by one third.

Star Struck

Roulades always look sophisticated and elegant – and this one is no exception. Carob and orange give it a classic effect.

Ingredients: Imperial/Metric

8oz/225g	wholemeal flour
3tsp	low sodium baking powder
1oz/25g	sugar
7tbsp	sesame seed oil
8fl oz/225ml	water
2	egg whites
1tbsp	carob powder
2	oranges (zest)
2 tsp	orange flower water
7oz/200g	*fromage frais*

Not Richard Proof
The roll up didn't quite work. The taste and texture were good but it didn't look the part.

Serves:	8
Calories:	239
Preparation Time:	20 minutes
Cooking Time:	20 minutes
Oven Temperature:	180°C, 350°F, Gas Mark 4

Can be frozen

Garnish:
8   carob fans
8   orange wings

Method:

1   Line a swiss-roll tin with lightly oiled greaseproof paper.
2   Sift the flour, carob powder and baking powder into a bowl.
3   Add the sugar, oil, water and egg whites and mix well.
4   Pour into the prepared tin and bake for about 20 minutes until the mixture is springy to the touch.
5   Meanwhile mix together the orange zest, orange flower water and *fromage frais*.
6   Once the roulade is cooked carefully turn it out onto a clean cloth covered with greaseproof paper. Peel off the old sheet of greaseproof paper and cover the roulade with a damp cloth. Leave to cool.
7   Spread the *fromage* mixture evenly over the roulade – not too thickly.
8   Using the new greaseproof paper lift and support the roulade and roll it up – so that it looks like a long swiss roll.
9   Serve chilled.

> **TIP BOX**
> The idea of the damp cloth is to keep the roulade moist – this way you can roll it up without it cracking.

Sweet Gingerbread Man

The lemon gives this ginger pudding an unusual tartness which is very pleasant. Molasses is a by-product of the sugar refining industry and is a rich source of nutrients. It is an excellent source of the B vitamins, iron and calcium. Blackstrap molasses is the most nutritious type you can purchase. The addition of molasses to the pudding gives it that nice 'sticky' quality that is essential for a true ginger pud.

Ingredients: Imperial/Metric

8oz/225g	wholemeal flour
3tsp	low sodium-baking powder
2tsp	ground ginger
1oz/25g	stem ginger, chopped
2tbsp	blackstrap molasses
1oz/25g	honey
3oz/75g	polyunsaturated, unhydrogenated margarine
3tbsp	soya milk
1	egg white
1	lemon (zest and juice)

Richard Proof

Serves:	8
Calories:	187
Preparation Time:	20 minutes
Cooking Time:	40 minutes
Oven Temperature:	170°C, 340°F, Gas Mark 4

Can be frozen

Method:

1. Lightly oil and line an 8in./20cm square baking tin.
2. Place the first four ingredients into a mixing bowl.
3. Heat the honey, molasses and margarine until the margarine has melted.
4. Combine all the ingredients together.
5. Mix well and pour into the prepared tin.
6. Bake until well-risen and golden brown.

TIP BOX
Store gingerbread in foil for a few days to make it 'stickier'.

Swap Shop Recipe
Staff of Life

Bread and butter pudding is Richard's absolute favourite – so it has to be good to gain his approval. This recipe is sweet without added sugar and it's nice and spicy.

 Richard Proof
Preparation Time: 20 minutes
Oven Temperature: 160°C, 325°F, Gas Mark 3
Can be frozen

Serves: 8
Cooking Time: 50 minutes

Traditional version		*Healthier version*	
Calories: 230		**Calories: 228**	
Ingredients: Imperial/Metric		**Ingredients:** Imperial/Metric	
9	slices white bread, crusts removed	9	slices wholemeal bread, crusts removed
3oz/75g	butter	2oz/50g	polyunsaturated unhydrogenated margarine
2oz/50g	sultanas	2oz/50g	sultanas
3oz/75g	sugar	2oz/50g	dried dates
4	eggs	4	egg whites
1¹/₂pt/600ml	full cream milk	1¹/₂pt/600ml	skimmed milk
1tsp	nutmeg	1tsp	freshly grated nutmeg

Method:
Spread the bread with the margarine and cut each slice into 4.
Arrange half in a lightly greased 2pt/1.2 litre oven-proof dish – dry side up.
Place the dates in a small pan with just enough water to cover and simmer for about 5 minutes until they are soft and pulpy. Mix the sultanas and dates together.
Place the sultana and date mixture on top of the bread. Cover with the remaining bread, dry side down.
Beat the egg whites and milk together and pour over the pudding.
Sprinkle the grated nutmeg over the top and bake for about 50 minutes until the top is golden.

> **TIP BOX**
> For an even fruitier pudding you can use fruited wholemeal bread instead of plain.

Ait-Skeiters

Angelica was known by countryfolk as 'Ait-Skeiters' because the children would use the hollow stem of the plant as a pea shooter and shoot oats through it. When angelica is added to fruit it reduces the tartness and thus is useful when you want to minimize the amount of sugar used. The crispy topping combined with the fruity base of this pudding gives it a lovely texture. And it's high in fibre too!

Ingredients: Imperial/Metric

8oz/225g	pears, washed and cored
8oz/225g	ripe cherries, washed and stoned
1	lemon (juice and zest)
2oz/50g	wholemeal breadcrumbs
2tbsp	honey
1oz/25g	sesame seeds
2oz/50g	oat bran flakes
1tsp	ground ginger
1tsp	ground cinnamon
2tbsp	fresh angelica, chopped

Richard Proof
Serves: 6
Calories: 130
Preparation Time: 25 minutes
Cooking Time: 25 minutes
Oven Temperature: 180°C, 350°F, Gas Mark 4

Can be frozen

Method:

1 Slice the pears and coat with the lemon juice.
2 Place the fruit and 1 tablespoon of angelica into the base of a shallow ovenproof dish.
3 Mix together the breadcrumbs, seeds, spices, honey, flakes and angelica.
4 Sprinkle this mixture over the fruit and bake for about 25 minutes until the top is crisp and golden.

Trumpet Keck

The stem of angelica is hollow and, as such, is a mock instrument which children blow down to make noises. Even today, angelica is known in many parts of the country as 'trumpet keck' because children use it as a crude kind of trumpet. Angelica adds a sweet, unique flavour to these light pancakes.

Ingredients: Imperial/Metric

1	egg white
5fl oz/150ml	orange juice
4fl oz/125ml	soft silken tofu
2oz/50g	oat bran flakes, crushed
3oz/75g	wholemeal flour
1	orange (zest)
1lb 2oz	strawberries, washed and hulled
4fl oz/125ml	*fromage frais*
1tbsp	chopped angelica

Richard Proof
Serves: 8
Calories: 91
Preparation Time: 15 minutes
Cooking Time: 15 minutes

Can be frozen

Method:

1   Mix the egg white, orange juice and tofu together in a liquidizer until smooth.
2   Add the crushed oat bran flakes and flour and blend until smooth. The mixture should be of a pouring consistency – if it isn't add a little more orange juice.
3   Very lightly oil a non-stick frying pan and gently heat it. Pour in about an eighth of the mixture and cook for about 2 minutes on both sides. Keep the pancakes warm under some foil while you cook the remainder.
4   Place half the strawberries in a liquidizer and blend until smooth.
5   Chop the remaining strawberries and place in a bowl with the *fromage frais*. Mix well.
6   Spoon some of the filling onto each pancake and fold into four – making a triangular shape.
7   Arrange on a serving dish.

> **TIP BOX**
> It's the stem of the angelica that you use to sweeten – the leaves taste bitter.

Striped Sensation

The vivid chocolate-brown and white stripes of this dessert look absolutely magnificent. The different textures and flavours will delight you and your guests. This treat looks better when served in tall-stemmed glasses.

Ingredients: Imperial/Metric

1qty	'Star Struck' base (see page 102)
11fl oz/300ml	low fat natural yoghurt
1	banana

Richard Proof

Serves:	6
Calories:	253
Preparation Time:	30 minutes
Cooking Time:	20 minutes
Oven Temperature:	180°C, 350°F, Gas Mark 4

Garnish

6   carob fans
6   sprigs of mint

Method:

1   Make the carob base as in the 'Star Struck' recipe but instead of rolling it up, make crumbs of it.
2   Mash the banana and mix with the yoghurt.
3   Divide one-third of the carob crumbs between the six glasses.
4   Next divide half the yoghurt mixture between the glasses.
5   Repeat the layers ending with a carob-crumb topping.
6   Garnish with a sprig of mint and a carob fan and serve.

Roman Ruin

The blackberry was renowned for its healing powers in ancient times. Anything – from a serpent's bite to mouth and throat disorders – was cured. Roman physicians also boiled the roots in wine and used the liquid as an astringent for wounds. The combination of blackberries and peaches gives this pie-like dessert an original flavour. Perfect to end a light meal – or on its own at tea time!

Ingredients: Imperial/Metric

1lb 2oz/500g	blackberries, washed and hulled
1lb 2oz/500g	peaches, skinned and sliced
4fl oz/125ml	orange juice
1tsp	ground cinnamon
4oz/125g	wholemeal flour
2oz/50g	oat bran flakes, crushed
2tsp	low-sodium baking powder
2tbsp	skimmed milk
1tbsp	sweet cicely, chopped
2oz/50g	polyunsaturated, unhydrogenated margarine

Richard Proof

Serves:	8
Calories:	167
Preparation Time:	20 minutes
Cooking Time:	20 minutes
Oven Temperature:	200°C, 400°F, Gas Mark 6

Can be frozen

Method:
1 Place the blackberries in a pan with the peaches and orange juice.
2 Simmer for about 5 minutes.
3 Stir in the cinnamon and transfer to an oven-proof dish.
4 Sift the flour and baking powder into a bowl and rub in the margarine until the mixture resembles fine breadcrumbs. Add the crushed flakes and chopped sweet cicely.
5 Blend in enough milk to make a fairly soft dough.
6 Turn out onto a lightly floured board and press to about 1cm thick.
7 Cut out shapes, using a scone or biscuit cutter, and arrange them on top of the fruit.
8 Brush with a little milk and bake for about 20 minutes, or until the topping is golden.

Emperor of the Garden

In China, the pumpkin is called 'emperor of the garden' and has become a symbol of fruitfulness. The pumpkin seeds in this dessert blend well with the greengages which are wonderfully sweet and therefore don't need any added sugar. The topping for this recipe is lovely and crunchy with a hint of spice – a nice range of textures and flavours.

Ingredients: Imperial/Metric

1lb 2oz/500g	greengages
4oz/100g	wholemeal bread-crumbs
4oz/100g	oat bran flakes
1tsp	mixed spice
1tbsp	pumpkin seeds
1tbsp	honey

Richard Proof

Serves:	6
Calories:	195
Preparation Time:	20 minutes
Cooking Time:	45 minutes
Oven Temperature:	180°C, 350°F, Gas Mark 4

Can be frozen

Method:
1 Wash and stone the greengages. Place in the base of an oven-proof dish.
2 Mix together the remaining ingredients and pile on top of the greengages.
3 Bake for about 45 minutes until the top is golden.

Wagon Wheels

These little rounds of carob and creamy *fromage frais* are wonderfully rich – especially when served with a carob sauce. They both look and taste really naughty – they will fool anyone!

Ingredients: Imperial/Metric

1qty	'Star Struck' base (see page 00)
11fl oz/300ml	*fromage frais*
5fl oz/150ml	low fat soft cheese
1tbsp	sugar-free apricot jam
2oz/50g	fresh apricots, skinned and stoned

Richard Proof

Serves:	4
Calories:	520
Preparation Time:	30 minutes
Cooking Time:	20 minutes
Chilling Time:	30 minutes
Oven Temperature:	180°C, 350°F, Gas Mark 4

Garnish:
3 carob quills
4 apricot halves, sliced

Method:

1   Make the 'Star Struck' base as directed. Leave to cool and cut into 8 equal rounds.

2   Mix together the *fromage frais*, soft cheese and jam.

3   Chop the apricots and add to the *fromage* mixture. Chill for 30 minutes.

4   Spread the *fromage* mixture onto four of the carob rounds and sandwich with the other round on top.

5   Garnish with the apricot slices and carob quills (see Tip Box on page 64).

Ever Decreasing Circles

When Richard throws a pebble into a stream, endless circles magically appear. My attempts just seem to plummet to the bottom of the stream without trace. These meringue rounds are reminiscent of the ever-decreasing circles.

Ingredients: Imperial/Metric

1qty	'Sweetheart' base (see page 54)
4oz/125g	sugar free carob bar
1tsp	honey
15fl oz/400ml	firm silken tofu, liquidized

Richard Proof

Serves:	8
Calories:	144
Preparation Time:	30 minutes
Cooking Time:	90 minutes
Oven Temperature:	150°C, 300°F, Gas Mark 2

Garnish

1oz/25g   melted carob

Method:

1   Make the meringue rounds as in 'Sweetheart'.

2   Break the carob into pieces and place in a small bowl with the honey. Stand over a pan of hot water and stir until melted.

3   Mix well together the tofu and carob.

4   Use three-quarters of the carob mixture to sandwich the rounds together. Garnish the top round with the remaining carob mixture and drizzle the carob on top of the rounds in a circular pattern.

TIP BOX

Never melt carob, or chocolate, over boiling water as the excess heat causes white specks to appear in the mixture.

Chapter Ten
Tempting Tarts

My mum makes the most wonderful pies and tarts that you could ever imagine. The pastry melts in the mouth and the fruit is always succulent and tasty – never pulpy. There was always a homemade tart in the pantry at home. Mum would always have a well stocked cupboard – just in case someone popped in. Nothing was wasted because my dad was always waiting, with a good appetite, in the wings – should no one call. Things are very much the same today. I have probably tasted more varieties of fruit tart in my time than most people and I certainly do enjoy them.

Richard is desperately boring in his taste for fruit tarts. His out-and-out favourite is apple and he doesn't like it 'tampered' with. I tend to get a little bored making a 'straight' apple tart and so I experiment by adding anything that just happens to be lying around the kitchen. Sometimes I get away with it and Richard, without realizing that I've pepped it up a little, will say how nice the tart is. I once added ground ginger and very finely chopped stem ginger and Richard thought that it was the best apple tart he had ever tasted. He did, that is, until I told him what was in it. It just goes to prove that it's all in the mind, doesn't it? I just don't tell Richard any more and as long as it looks like apple he'll love it.

A classic apple tart I made a few years ago had green tomatoes in it – just to keep the apples company. We had grown these tomatoes and they just wouldn't ripen and so I added a few to this tart. That's one time I didn't get away with pulling the wool over Richard's eyes. I must admit that it had a quite unusual taste – to say the very least.

Personally I like to taste something a little different to the normal run-of-the-mill tarts. Whilst I am quite happy with apple tart I do prefer something like 'Starry Starry Night' or 'Allo Allo'. Different textures and flavours are important to me. Home-made tarts are always eaten in our little hen pen – my dad and Richard see to that!

With the fat and flour of the pastry and the sugar in the filling tarts are quite heavy on the calories. Quite often shop bought tarts have so much sugar in them that the filling tastes just like a sugar syrup – and the fruit could be absolutely anything. In fact, my mum used to tell me that during the war people used to make fruit pies with turnip because fruit was so rare. As fat was virtually unobtainable to make the pastry cream crackers were used for the pie crust. It makes apple pie sound marvellous, doesn't it? To enhance the natural sweetness of the fruit I tend to use fruit juice instead of sugar. Fruit such as bananas, dates and sultanas, which have a naturally high sugar content can be added to any tart to sweeten in lieu of sugar. By doing this you not only reduce the calories and increase the nutrients but you bring out the fruit flavour as well.

The fat content of my pastry is reduced considerably by using yeast to 'lighten' the mixture. Most people will have experienced nasty moments using wholemeal pastry as it can be difficult to handle. Not this one. This pastry is not only low in fat and calories but it handles very easily. You will never break this pastry when rolling it out nor will it disintegrate into a pile of crumbs. It is pliable and very easy to manage – even Richard uses it. For a change I add different kinds of fruit zest to the pastry – orange, lime, lemons and grapefruit can all be used successfully. This addition really gives a nice 'kick' to the pastry and also continues the fruit theme throughout the whole dessert.

The variety of fruit tarts is endless and they do freeze extremely well. It's certainly worth stocking up your freezer and taking advantage of fruit in surplus supply. And, to ring the changes, you can make open lattice tarts, single-crust tarts, individual tarts and 'shaped' tarts. I'm planning a surprise 'shaped' tart for our fifteenth wedding anniversary meal next week. Little heart-shaped lattice topped tarts with an apple and passion fruit base – it can't fail, can it?

La Patisserie

The special feature of this particular pastry recipe is its very low fat content. Yeast is used to 'lighten' the pastry a little and, as a result, only 25g of fat is used – that's a considerable reduction.

Ingredients: Imperial/Metric

6oz/175g	wholemeal flour, plain
$\frac{1}{2}$ tsp	easy-blend dried yeast
1	egg white, beaten
1fl oz/25ml	sunflower oil
5tbsp	water
pinch	vitamin C powder

Not Richard Proof

He just couldn't get the hang of kneading at first – too light-handed with it. As a result the pastry was too heavy.

Serves:	plenty for one pie
Calories for the recipe:	790
Preparation time:	15 minutes
Can be frozen	

Method:
1 Mix the flour, yeast and vitamin C in a bowl.
2 Add the egg white.
3 Place the oil and water in a small pan and heat. Do not allow this liquid to become too hot. When warm, add to the flour mixture.
4 Form the dough into a ball and knead for 5 minutes. Then leave to rest under a clean tea towel until you are ready to use it.

> **TIP BOX**
> By simply adding 3 teaspoons of fruit zest to this pastry you can transform the taste. Orange, lemon, lime and grapefruit are all delicious variations.

112

Tutti Frutti

These little tartlets just melt in the mouth – you can't restrict yourself to eating one. They are perfect for buffet–style dinners and parties and are a boon for the picnic hamper. Alive with colour, they will enhance any occasion.

Ingredients: Imperial/Metric

1qty	'La Patisserie' (see page 112) lime flavour
2tbsp	sugar-free apricot jam
2tbsp	sugar-free redcurrant jelly
1tbsp	lemon juice
12oz	prepared fresh fruits (strawberries, raspberries, grapes, cherries, tangerines, etc.)

Richard Proof

Serves:	8
Calories:	122
Preparation Time:	40 minutes
Cooking Time:	20 minutes
Chilling Time:	30 minutes
Oven Temperature:	200°C, 400°F, Gas Mark 6

Can be frozen

Garnish:

1   sprigs of mint

Method:

1   Roll out the pastry and line eight 3in./7.5cm tartlet tins. Bake blind for 10 minutes until golden brown. Cool.

2   Stir the redcurrant jelly with half the lemon juice in a pan over a low heat until the mixture is fully blended. Do the same with the apricot jam and the second half of the juice.

3   Strain each through a nylon sieve and allow to cool slightly.

4   Using the jelly for the red fruits and the apricot jam for the yellow, orange and green fruits, brush the bases of the pastry cases with the glaze.

5   Arrange the fruits on top and brush with the glaze. Allow to set before serving.

TIP BOX
Any red and yellow jams can be used and the variety of sugar-free jam is now quite good.

Swap Shop Recipe
A Christmas Carol

We always have mincemeat tarts in our house at Christmastime, and over the New Year. It just wouldn't be Christmas without them. Traditional mincemeat contains lots of sugar and suet – neither of which are really needed. The dried fruits provide enough sweetness, and the addition of grated carrot adds the moisture. My version is far tastier than the traditional tarts and benefits from being healthier and less calorific. This mincemeat will keep for about a week if you store it in the refrigerator – it never has in our house though!

Richard Proof
Preparation Time: 40 minutes
Oven Temperature: 200°C, 400°F, Gas Mark 6

Serves:　　10
Cooking Time: 40 minutes
Can be frozen

Traditional version		*Healthier version*	
Calories: 867		Calories : 334	
Ingredients: Imperial/Metric		**Ingredients**: Imperial/Metric	
Mincemeat:		*Mincemeat*:	
8oz/225g	currants	8oz/225g	currants
8oz/225g	sultanas	8oz/225g	sultanas
1lb/450g	grated apple	1lb/450g	grated apple
4oz/125g	candied peel	3tbsp	fruit zest from oranges, limes, lemons & grapefruit
2oz/50g	*glacé* cherries	2oz/50g	dried dates, chopped
12oz/350g	sugar		not required
12oz/350g	shredded suet	8oz/225g	grated carrot
4tbsp	brandy	4tbsp	brandy or orange juice
1tsp	grated nutmeg	1tsp	grated nutmeg
$\frac{1}{2}$tsp	cinnamon	$\frac{1}{2}$tsp	cinnamon
1tsp	ground ginger	1tsp	ground ginger
2oz/50g	flaked almonds	2oz/50g	flaked almonds
Pastry:		*Pastry*:	
9oz	plain white flour	2qty	Lemon-flavoured 'La Patisserie' (see page 112)
2tbsp	water		
5oz/150g	butter		
1tbsp	caster sugar		
1	egg yolk		

Method

Line a 9in./23cm tart tin with three-quarters of the pastry – rolled out thinly.

Spoon in the mincemeat filling. Dampen the edges of the pastry. Roll out the remaining pastry and cover the tart.

Trim the edges and bake for about 40 minutes until the top is a light golden brown.

You can make individual tarts if you prefer – why not try some shaped like Christmas trees?

Alexander The Great

Legend has it that a circle of date palms was planted by one of the generals serving under Alexander the Great over two thousand years ago – and it still bears fruit to this day. The sweetness in this recipe is produced by the dates and a little honey. And if you like rhubarb pies this is the tart for you.

Ingredients: Imperial/Metric

1qty	'La Patisserie' (see page 112)
1tbsp	honey
1oz/25g	oat bran
1lb/450g	rhubarb, washed and trimmed
2oz/50g	dried dates, pitted
4fl oz/125ml	low fat natural yoghurt

Richard Proof

Serves:	6
Calories:	195
Preparation Time:	30 minutes
Cooking Time:	25 minutes
Oven Temperature:	200°C, 400°F, Gas Mark 6

Can be frozen

Method:
1 Line a 10in./25cm tart tin with the pastry.
2 Warm the honey slightly and add to the oat bran. Spread this mixture over the pastry base.
3 Cut the rhubarb into 1in./2.5cm lengths and spread evenly over the oat mixture.
4 Place the dates in a small pan with just enough water to cover and simmer for about 5 minutes. The dates should be soft and pulpy.
5 Spoon the date mixture over the rhubarb and pour the yoghurt on top.
6 Bake until the topping just starts to turn brown in places.
7 Serve either hot or cold.

Tops and Tails

Blackcurrants and oranges are a classic combination carried right through to the pastry which has orange zest in it. Blackcurrants are a high-fibre fruit because you eat all the seeds. The addition of the wholemeal breadcrumbs and dates boosts the fibre content still further. I don't know about you, but I hate topping and tailing fruit – it seems to be endless.

Ingredients: Imperial/Metric

2qty	'La Patisserie', orange flavoured (see page 112)
1lb/450g	blackcurrants, washed, topped and tailed
2oz/50g	dried dates, pitted
2oz/50g	wholemeal breadcrumbs
1	orange (zest and juice)

Richard Proof

Serves:	8
Calories:	139
Preparation Time:	30 minutes
Cooking Time:	30 minutes
Oven Temperature:	150°C, 300°F, Gas Mark 2

Can be frozen

Method:

1 Line a 10in./25cm tart tin with three-quarters of the pastry.
2 Cook the blackcurrants in a little water until they are fairly soft.
3 Chop the dates finely and add to the blackcurrants with the orange juice and zest.
4 Add the breadcrumbs.
5 Fill the pastry case with the mixture.
6 Roll out the remaining pastry until it is quite thin and cut into long strips – about 1cm in width. Make a lattice pattern on the top of the pie with the strips by criss-crossing them. You can buy lattice cutters from most kitchen shops and they do save both time and effort. And, they're quite cheap!
7 Bake until the pastry is crisp and golden.

TIP BOX

To reduce the calories in a tart don't use both the top and bottom crust – just use one or the other.

116

Sultan's Surprise

This unusual combination of bananas and mincemeat works extremely well. The sweet, mellow and creamy quality of the banana gives a nice contrast to the crunchy, tart nature of the mincemeat.

Ingredients: Imperial/Metric

1qty	'La Patisserie' (see page 112)
2oz/50g	polyunsaturated, unhydrogenated, margarine
1oz/25g	sugar
2	egg whites
2oz/50g	ground sesame seeds
2tsp	almond essence
4tbsp	sugar-and fat-free mincemeat
2	bananas, sliced thinly

Garnish

1oz/25g	flaked almonds

Richard Proof

Serves:	6
Calories:	317
Preparation Time:	30 minutes
Cooking Time:	30 minutes
Oven Temperature:	200°C, 400°F, Gas Mark 6

Can be frozen

> **TIP BOX**
> Both baked and unbaked pastry freezes very well.

Method

1 Line a 10in./25cm pie dish with the pastry.
2 Cream the margarine and sugar together and stir in the beaten egg whites, ground seeds and almond essence. Mix well.
3 Fill the pie dish nearly to the top with alternate layers of mincemeat and banana.
4 Spread the mincemeat over the top and scatter with the flaked almonds.
5 Bake until golden brown in colour.

Starry Starry Night

This is a very rich dessert which has a pastry layer, a creamy layer and a fruit topping. You can use any variety of fruit which happens to be about at the time. I particularly like star fruit because it looks so attractive when sliced – and the strawberries add a nice burst of colour. You don't need large portions of this unusual tart as it is very filling.

Ingredients: Imperial/Metric

1qty	'La Patisserie' (see page 112)
4oz/125g	ground sunflower seeds
5fl oz/150ml	water
2	oranges (zest)
4	drops of almond essence
1	star fruit, washed
8oz/225g	strawberries, washed

Richard Proof

Serves:	6
Calories:	257
Preparation Time:	40 minutes
Cooking Time:	25 minutes
Oven Temperature:	190°C, 375°F, Gas Mark 5

Method:

1 Line an 8in./20cm tart tin with the pastry, prick the base and cook for 5 minutes.
2 Mix the ground seeds, water, orange zest and almond essence together. Spoon into the tart tin. Bake for about 20 minutes.
3 Slice the star fruit thinly and arrange in the centre part of the tart.
4 Do not hull the strawberries; make strawberry fans and place around the edge of the tart.

The Flying Stork

I decided to add lime juice and zest to the gooseberries in this recipe just to see what the result would be. Everyone approves of this unusual combination!

Ingredients: Imperial/Metric

1lb/450g	gooseberries
3tbsp	apple juice
1	lime (zest and juice)
1qty	'La Patisserie', lime flavoured (see page 112)

Richard Proof

Serves:	6
Calories:	159
Preparation Time:	30 minutes
Cooking Time:	25 minutes
Oven Temperature:	200°C, 400°F, Gas Mark 6

Can be frozen

Method:

1 Cook the gooseberries gently with the apple juice until fairly soft.
2 Add the lime juice and zest. Leave to one side to cool slightly.
3 Line a 10in./25cm tart tin with two-thirds of the pastry rolled out very thinly.
4 Pour in the gooseberry mixture.
5 Roll out the remaining pastry and cover the tart, trim the edges and bake until golden brown.

TIP BOX

Gooseberries are one of the first fruits to make an appearance in the spring and are great to stock up on because they freeze well.

Swap Shop Recipe
Pozo

The upturned cherries which cover this tart remind me of those big red noses that clowns wear. My favourite clown is called Pozo and I came across him whilst reading *Waiting for Godot* – I've never forgotten him.

Richard Proof
Preparation Time: 35 minutes
Oven Temperature: 200°C, 400°F, Gas Mark 6

Serves: 6
Cooking Time: 25 minutes
Can be frozen

Traditional version

Calories: 776

Ingredients: Imperial/Metric
Pastry:

9oz/250g	plain white flour
5oz/150g	butter
2tbsp	caster sugar
2	egg yolks
2tbsp	cold water

Filling:

6	drops almond essence
3oz/75g	sugar
2oz/50g	ground almonds
3oz/75g	caster sugar
4	egg yolks
2tbsp	plain white flour
2tbsp	cornflour
11fl oz/300ml	full cream milk
3	drops vanilla essence
1lb 2oz/500g	dessert cherries
6oz/175g	redcurrant jelly
2tbsp	water

Healthier version

Calories: 193

Ingredients: Imperial/Metric
Pastry:

1qty	'La Patisserie', orange flavoured, (see page 112)

Filling:

2	large cooking apples, peeled and cored
3tbsp	apple juice
1lb 2oz/500g	dessert cherries, washed and stoned
1tbsp	honey

Method:
Line an 8in./20cm tart tin with the pastry. Bake blind (see Tip Box on page 120) for 20 minutes.
Chop the apples and place in a pan with the apple juice. Simmer gently until the apples are a pulpy mixture.
Spoon this mixture into the tart tin. Arrange the cherries, cut side down, on top of the apple mixture until the surface is covered.
Gently heat the honey and brush over the cherries. Serve cold.

Allo, Allo,

I have based this recipe on a classical French number commonly known as 'glazed apple tart'. The confectioners' custard has been replaced with a purée of apples and apricots which not only makes the dish healthier but tastes far nicer as well.

Ingredients: Imperial/Metric

1qty	'La Patisserie' (see page 112)
2	large cooking apples
9oz/250g	apricots, skinned, stoned and chopped
1lb/450g	eating apples, washed
3tbsp	apple juice
1tbsp	honey

Richard Proof

Serves:	8
Calories:	134
Preparation Time:	35 minutes
Cooking Time:	30 minutes
Oven Temperature:	200°C, 400°F, Gas Mark 6

Can be frozen

Method:

1 Line a 9in./23cm tart tin with the pastry, prick the base and bake blind for 5 minutes.
2 Peel and core the cooking apples and place in a pan with the apricots and apple juice.
3 Cover and poach for about 10 minutes. Purée in a liquidizer until fairly smooth. Spoon the mixture into the tart tin.
4 Core the eating apples and thinly slice. Arrange the pieces in a circular pattern, slightly overlapping each other until the whole surface area is covered.
5 Bake for about 20 minutes. Cool slightly.
6 Melt the honey and brush over the fruit. Serve hot or cold.

Chapter Eleven
Saucy Toppers

Sauces made with fresh fruit or dried fruit can transform the most mundane dessert into something special. What I like to do is pour one or two contrasting sauces around the base of individual desserts and then make star or spiral patterns in it with yoghurt. The effect is stunning and yet only takes a minute to achieve. It's certainly worth the little bit of time and effort involved. I very rarely serve a sauce in a jug separately because it doesn't show it off to its fullest effect.

The beauty about sauces is that they are so quick and easy to make – you can whip one up in minutes. You can make a sauce out of any fruit and it will be a success. And, what's more, sauces freeze well, which means that you can stock up your freezer when seasonal fruits are very cheap. I must admit that I am a sauce fanatic. I love them drizzled over a pudding, around an individual tart or even on their own!

Most sauces that are served in restaurants or bought in packets from a supermarket, do not resemble the homemade varieties at all. For one thing they will be loaded with sugar and taste nothing like the fruit they are supposed to contain. The over-riding flavour is one of sugar syrup. I tend to use either honey or fruit juice to enhance the real fruit flavour. Most of the time the fruit itself is sweet enough and needs no help.

Cream and egg yolks often find their way into sauces and you can easily substitute tofu, yoghurt and potato flour for them instead. These simple minor changes will not only improve the taste of the sauces but will make them healthy and substantially reduce the calorie content.

Merlin's Magic

My favourite sauce in particular is this one. The aroma is pungent and the flavour strong. The combination of mango and passion fruit is magic – Merlin himself couldn't have conjured up anything to match this . . .

Ingredients: Imperial/Metric
8oz/225g   mango
2   passion fruit
4fl oz/125ml fresh orange juice

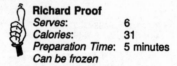

Richard Proof
Serves: 6
Calories: 31
Preparation Time: 5 minutes
Can be frozen

Method
1 Peel the mango and cut the flesh from the large flat central stone.
2 Scoop out the flesh and seeds from the passion fruit.
3 Place all the ingredients in a liquidizer and blend until smooth.
4 Serve slightly chilled.

Abraham's Sauce

According to legend an angel let the prophet Abraham into the secrets of making yoghurt. Abraham lived until he was 175 years of age and was said to have fathered a child when he was 100 years *young*! This creamy red sauce is the perfect topping for ice cream, or garnish for mousses! Its bright colour makes it fun to work with. Why not try making swirls in fresh low fat yoghurt as a sumptuous, low calorie treat.

Ingredients: Imperial/Metric
8oz/225g   ripe cherries
10tbsp   water
2tbsp   red grape juice
4tbsp   low fat natural yoghurt

Richard Proof
Serves: 6
Preparation Time: 10 minutes
Cooking Time: 15 minutes
Can be frozen

Method:
1 Wash the cherries, remove the stalks and stones. Place in a covered sauce-pan with the water and heat gently.
2 Place in a liquidizer with the grape juice and blend until smooth.
3 Allow to cool before stirring in the yoghurt.
4 Chill before use.

Swap Shop Recipe
Climbing Orchid

Vanilla comes from the pod of a climbing orchid and originates from Central America. This sauce is very rich and fairly thick – perfect for coating desserts.

Richard Proof
Preparation Time: 10 minutes
Chilling time: 30 minutes

Serves: 4
Cooking Time: 5 minutes
Can be frozen

Traditional version

Calories: 394

Ingredients: Imperial/Metric

10fl oz/250ml	double cream
2oz/50g	plain chocolate
2oz/50g	sugar
2 drops	vanilla essence

Healthier version

Calories: 81

Ingredients: Imperial/Metric

10fl oz/250ml	low fat natural yoghurt
2oz/50g	sugar–free carob bar
$\frac{1}{2}$tbsp	honey, heated
2 drops	vanilla essence

Method:
Break up the carob and place in a small bowl over a pan of hot water and stir until melted.
Mix together the yoghurt, honey, vanilla essence and carob.
Leave to cool in the refrigerator.

Strawberry Fair

This is one or Richard's favourite sauces – he loves it on ice cream. The tart flavour of the strawberries enhances any sweet dessert.

Ingredients: Imperial/Metric

8oz/225g	strawberries, washed and hulled
1tbsp	concentrated apple and strawberry juice

Richard Proof
Serves: 6
Calories: 20
Preparation Time: 5 minutes
Can be frozen

Method:
1 Place the strawberries in a liquidizer with the juice and blend until smooth.
2 Press through a sieve and serve.

Yellow Brick Road

Dried apricots make wonderful sauces – tasty and rich. You can add some fresh chopped apricots to the liquidized sauce when they are in season. This sauce is a perfect addition to sorbets or ice creams.

Ingredients: Imperial/Metric

4oz/125g	dried apricots
1¹/₂pt/600ml	water
1tbsp	honey
1	lemon (zest and juice)

Richard Proof
Serves: 6
Calories: 75
Preparation Time: 10 minutes
Cooking Time: 15 minutes
Can be frozen

Method:

1 Soak the apricots overnight in the water.
2 Place the apricots, with their soaking liquid, in a pan and simmer for 15 minutes.
3 Add the honey, lemon zest and juice.
4 Blend the mixture in a liquidizer until fairly smooth.
5 Serve either hot or cold.

Houdini

Crème de Cassis is a liqueur made from blackcurrants, sugar and alcohol. There are no additives, flavourings or colourings added. As it's sweet, it is useful to combine with fruits because you benefit from the natural flavour. Richard named this sauce 'Houdini' because when he'd made this sauce it couldn't escape from the jug!

Ingredients: Imperial/Metric

6oz/175g	fresh blackberries
1tbsp	Crème de Cassis
¹/₂tsp	potato flour
1tbsp	cold water

Not Richard Proof
Guess what? He did it again – forgot to stir the mixture continuously. It was lumpy again.

Serves: 4
Calories: 25
Preparation Time: 5 minutes
Can be frozen

Method:

1 Wash the blackberries and liquidize them. Place in a sieve and press through into a saucepan. Heat very gently.
2 Add the Crème de Cassis and stir in.
3 Mix the potato flour with the water to make a smooth paste. Add to the liquid. Stir continuously until the mixture thickens.
4 Serve when warmed through.

Strawberry Blonde

Can you remember the old James Cagney film where he, as the character Biff Grimes, bribes the band to play 'Strawberry Blonde' as he dances with his new blonde girlfriend? What a marvellous film that was – they don't make them like that any more. And you might think the same about this creamy sauce!

Ingredients: Imperial/Metric
8oz/225g   strawberries
5fl oz/150ml   soft silken tofu
1tbsp   apple and stawberry concentrate

Richard Proof
Serves: 6
Calories: 31
Preparation Time: 5 minutes
Can be frozen

Method:

1 Wash and hull the strawberries.
2 Place all the ingredients in the liquidizer and blend until smooth.

Apollo

The bright orange colour of this sauce reminds me of the sunshine we sometimes experience in the height of summer. As Apollo is the Greek god of the sun I thought this an apt name for the recipe.

Ingredients: Imperial/Metric
4   tangerines
11fl oz/300ml   orange juice
2tsp   potato flour

Not Richard Proof
Richard didn't stir the mixture when heating it which resulted in a very lumpy sauce.

Serves: 6
Calories: 26
Preparation Time: 10 minutes
Cooking Time: 5 minutes
Can be frozen

Method:

1 Mix the potato flour with a little orange juice and blend to a smooth paste.
2 Pour the remaining orange juice into a small pan and heat gently.
3 Remove the zest from the tangerines, peel and segment them. Add to the pan.
4 Stir in the potato flour paste and continue to stir until it begins to thicken.
5 Serve warm.

TIP BOX
A lot of fibre is contained in the membrane which surrounds the segments of tangerines and other citrus fruit. I retain it wherever possible.

Swap Shop Recipe
Whiter Shade of Pale

This fluffy sauce has the consistency of whipped cream – try it with a combination of other sauces or as a garnish or creamy topping for cakes and tarts.

 Richard Proof   *Serves*: 4   *Preparation Time*: 5 minutes

Traditional version		*Healthier version*	
Calories: 465		Calories: 103	
Ingredients: Imperial/Metric		**Ingredients:** Imperial/Metric	
11fl oz/300ml	double cream	11fl oz/300ml	Greek strained yoghurt
4oz/125g	sugar		not needed
1	egg white	1	egg white

Method:
Beat the egg white until stiff and gently fold into the yoghurt.

Red Zinger

This sauce is a rich, deep red in colour and has a very strong flavour. Its delicious on plain yoghurt or mousses.

Ingredients: Imperial/Metric
1lb/450g	raspberries
2tbsp	apple and raspberry concentrate

Richard Proof
Serves: 6
Calories: 38
Preparation Time: 10 minutes
Cooking Time: 15 minutes
Can be frozen

Method:
1. Wash the raspberries and place them in a pan with the concentrate.
2. Heat gently until the fruit starts to break up a little.
3. Rub through a sieve and serve hot or cold.

> **TIP BOX**
> Why not try this sauce frozen in alternate layers with ice cream. When the mixture is scooped out you get a stunning ripple effect.

Index

Aaron's Rod   42
Abraham's Sauce   122
agar   14
Ait-Skeiters   105
Alexander the Great   115
Allo, Allo,   120
angelica   18, 105, 106
Apollo   125
Apple John   54–5
apples:
    filo fancies   79
    fruit salads   50, 51, 54–5, 56
    ice cream   91
    mousses and fools   31, 38–9
    puddings   98, 99
    tarts   120
apricots:
    dried   33
    recipes   32–3, 48, 120, 124
Arabian Nights   77
Archangel's Wings   50–1

baking powder 14
Bali Sunrise 65
bananas:
    recipes   29, 30, 43, 67–8, 78, 93, 106,
        117
    ripeness   43
Bangkok Beauty   90
Bedouin   51
Bells of St Clements   28
bilberries: recipes   36, 60–1, 77
biscuits: crushing 73
Bishop's Mitres   47
blackberries: recipes   54–5, 91, 107,
    124
blackcurrants: recipes   37, 116
Blushing Bride   31–2
bombes   88–9

Bougatsa   82
Bramble   37
bread and butter pudding   104

caffeine   19
carob   13–14
    fans   35
    recipes   29, 35, 57, 63, 87, 102, 109,
        123
Cashbags   76
Cassia   66
Cassis   91
Catherine Wheels   78
Chaffey   32–3
cheese, low fat soft   15
cheesecakes   59–74
    freezing   74
cherries: recipes   43, 81, 105, 119, 122
chestnuts: recipe   83
cholesterol   2–3, 5
Christmas Carol   114–15
Christmas Cracker   100–1
cinnamon   18
clementines: recipe   48
Climbing Orchid   123
coffee   19
conversion tables   22–3
courgettes: recipe   101

damsons: recipe   33–4
dates   51
Days of Wine and Roses   45

eggs   20
eggs: whisking   25–6
Emperor of the Garden   108
Ever Decreasing Circles   109
exercise   7
Exotica   56

fats   6, 16–17
   saturated   2, 5
fibre   2, 5, 6
figs: recipes   48, 51, 56
filo pastry   20, 75–6
   deserts with   76–84
   thawing   78
flour   14
Fluted Fancies   57
Flying Stork   118
Food of the Pharaohs   46
fools   25–6, 27, 30, 31–2
fromage frais   15
Frosty the Snowman   87
fruit   18–19
   cooking   46
   dried   119
      recipes   46, 76, 84, 100–1, 114
   freezing   25
   fresh   41
   salads   41–57
   as sweeteners   25
   sweetening   111
   washing   69
fruit juices: as sweeteners 17–18

gelatin   14
gelozone   15
gingerbread pudding   103
gooseberries: recipes   98, 118
grapefruit: recipe   50
grapes: recipes   42, 50, 52–3
Great Wall of China   69
greengages:
   recipes   30, 69, 77, 108
Greensleeves   31

Hades and Minthe   63–4
heart disease   1–3, 6–7
Hedgehog   55
herbs:
   with fruit   25
   as sweeteners   18
High Balls   40
Hippocrates   48
honey   18
Houdini   124
Huckleberry Finn   60–1

ice cream   85–6, 92, 93–5
   bombes   88–9
   recipes   87, 89, 90–1
   ripple effect   91
ice houses   85
iced desserts   85–95
Iced Dream   92

ingredients: healthy and unhealthy 10–13
Isle of Honey   52–3

Jolly Green Giant   101
Jolly Jesters   44
Jolly Miner   98

Karyon   62–3
King of Hearts   84
kiwi fruit: recipes   43, 50, 55, 69, 88
kumquats: recipes   47, 48, 56, 81

lemon: twists   38
Limey   30
lychees: recipes   47, 48, 50, 56

Magic Carpet   26
mango: recipes   39, 55, 73–4, 90, 122
Marco Polo   50
Marron   83
Medicine Tree   86–7
melons: recipe   50
meringues   109
Merlin's Magic   122
Mesopotamia   43
Metchnikoff   34
milk   15–16
mincemeat tarts   114–15, 117
Mistral   67
mousses   25–6, 28, 30–5, 39–40
Mrs Miniver   80
My Darling Clementine   48–9

New Zealand Sunset   88

Oat Cuisine   73–4
oats   19–20, 65
oils   17
Old Hat   79
oranges: recipes   28, 32, 90, 102, 116
oven temperatures   23

pancakes   105–6
papaya:
   recipes   48, 50, 56, 86–7
   seeds   48
Party Piece   94
Passion   30
passion fruit: recipes   30, 47, 48, 56, 81,
   122
pastry:
   baking blind   120
   fat content   112
   filo, *see* filo pastry
   flavouring   112
   recipe   112

Patisserie, (La) 112
pavlova 54
peaches:
  peeling 34
  recipes 34, 47, 50, 77–8, 90–1, 107
pears: recipes 53, 105
pectin 39
Pillow Talk 77–8
pineapple: recipe 42
Pink Panther 36
Policeman's Helmet 88–9
Pot Pourri 72–3
Pozo 119
prunes: recipes 26, 40, 89
Pucker Up 27
puddings 97–109
Punch and Judy 33–4

quark 15

raspberries: recipes 37, 42, 71, 91, 92,
  126
Red Ice 92
Red Zinger 126
Red-hot Pokers 53
redcurrants: recipes 37, 77
rhubarb:
  cooking 27
  recipes 27, 115
Roman Ruin 107

St John's Bread 29
St Valentines 71
salt 2, 5, 6
sauces 121–30
  serving 121
Scarb Jackets 99
semolina: recipe 82
setting agents 14–15
Shades of Summer 95
Soft and Silky 90–1
Solomon's Nectar 70–1
sorbets 85, 86–7, 88, 90, 92
Spice of Life 32
Staff of Life 104
star fruit: recipes 47, 56, 81, 117–18
Star is Born 81
Star Struck 102
Starry Starry Night 117–18
steamed puddings: cooking 97
strawberries:
  carob cups 57
  cheesecake 73–4
  fans 55
  filo fancies 77–8, 80
  fool 31–2

fruit salads 43, 55
ice cream 95
pudding 105–6
rinsing 32
sauces 123, 125
tarts 117–18
Strawberry Blonde 125
Strawberry Fair 123
Striped Sensation 106
strudel pastry, see filo pastry
sugar 2, 5, 6, 17
Sultan's Surprise 117
Surprise Delight 89
sweet cicely 18
Sweet Gingerbread Man 103
sweeteners 17–18
Sweetheart 54
syllabubs 32–3, 38

Taj Mahal 39
tangerines: recipes 42, 125
tarts 111–20
Tenerife Temptation 93
tofu 13, 25
Tops and Tails 116
Tropicana 67–8
Trumpet Keck 105–6
Tutti Frutti 113
Twenty-two Carat 35

vitamins: from fruit 18–19

Wagon Wheels 108–9
walnuts: recipe 62
watermelon ice cream 92
White Nun 38
Whiter Shade of Pale 126

Yellow Brick Road 124
yoghurt 15